Letters And Numbers For Me

_____

Print Child's Name

by Jan Z. Olsen, OTR
Developer of the Handwriting Without Tears® curriculum

Handwriting Without Tears®

Jan Z. Olsen, OTR

8001 MacArthur Blvd
Cabin John, MD 20818
Tel: 301–263–2700 ▪ Fax: 301–263–2707
www.hwtears.com ▪ JanOlsen@hwtears.com

Welcome!

Hi and welcome to the Handwriting Without Tears® (HWT) method. I'm Jan Olsen, the developer of the program. I'm an occupational therapist and have specialized in handwriting for more than 25 years. Handwriting Without Tears® is a simple, developmentally based method of teaching that makes handwriting easy to learn.

My interest in handwriting came from helping my own son who had printing problems in the first grade. Since then, I have worked with children, parents, teachers, and therapists to help them learn the unique and helpful features of the Handwriting Without Tears® program. Every year, millions of students use the program. They find it easy and fun and the results are very satisfying.

The purpose of my work is to make handwriting available to children as an automatic, natural skill. I know that children who write well and easily do better in school, enjoy their classes more and feel proud of themselves.

Introduction to
Letters and Numbers for Me

A child should practice a little each day. Five minutes is fine. Do not worry about finishing the page.

Before using this workbook, read *Handwriting Without Tears Teacher's Guide*. It will show you how to use the Wood Pieces Set for Capital Letters, the Capital Letter Cards, the Mat, the HWT Slate Chalkboard, and this student workbook.

Capital letters give the best start! Teach them first and stay with them until they are mastered. The time you spend on capitals is the foundation for handwriting success.

Demonstrate! Read the directions out loud to your students. Show each letter, step-by-step. Check each child's letter formation.

Every child can be successful with numbers! Use the unique wet–dry–try method on the slate chalkboard to prevent reversals and to make numbers a joy to learn. Present the HWT gray blocks as pictures of the slate. Teach numbers at any time, but always in numerical order.

Finally, this workbook can be individualized. You may teach letters out of order for specific purposes (such as teaching the letters in a child's name). Encourage children to draw and color in the book.

TABLE OF CONTENTS

Back of Book

i

Suggested Pencil Grip and Posture

Left-Handed Students

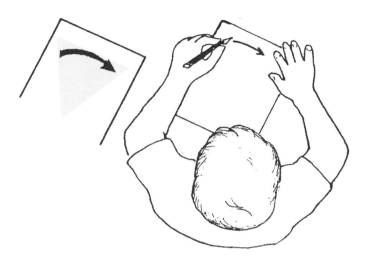

Place the top left corner of the paper higher for left-handed students.

Right-Handed Students

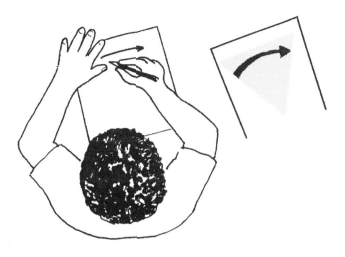

Place the top right corner of the paper higher for right-handed students.

Alternate Grip

Place the pencil between the thumb pad and index finger pad. The pencil rests on the middle finger. The eraser points back toward the shoulder of the writing hand.

An alternate grip is a pinch with the thumb and two fingers. The pencil rests on the ring finger.

Alternate Grip

Capitals, Numbers, and Lowercase Letters

1

CAPITAL LETTERS FOR ME

Teach Capital Letters First

Children love capital letters! All capital letters start at the same place — the TOP! Starting at the top is a very important habit. Capital letters are so easy to recognize and write. They use four basic strokes: big lines, little lines, big curves and little curves. Capital letters are the same height. They are big, bold and familiar!
You may alter the order for teaching letters to meet the needs of your class or curriculum.

Frog Jump Capital Letters

Start in the "starting corner" (top left). Make a "big line" down.
Frog Jump back to the "starting corner" and finish the letter.

F   E   D   P   B   R   N   M

Starting Corner Capital Letters

Start in the "starting corner" (top left). The first group begins with a "big line."

H   K   L

Diagonal lines are difficult. Teachers may reserve them for later and skip ahead to the Center Starters.

U   V   W   X   Y   Z

Center Starter Capital Letters

Start at the top center.
The first group begins with a "Magic C."

C   O   Q   G

The second group includes:

S   A   I   T   J

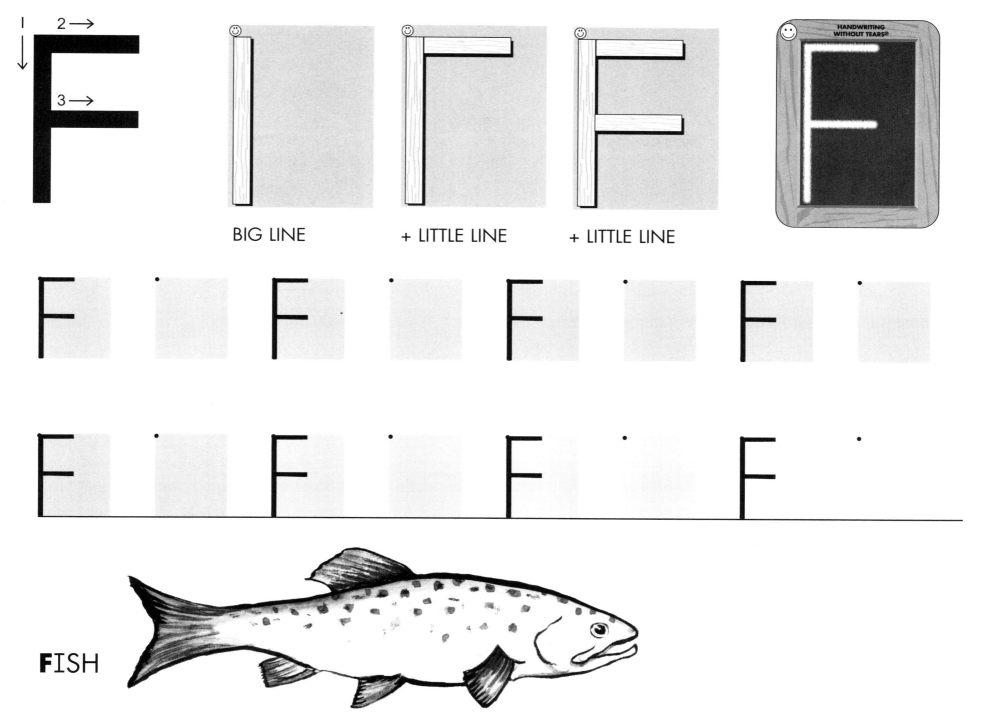

BIG LINE   + LITTLE LINE   + LITTLE LINE

FISH

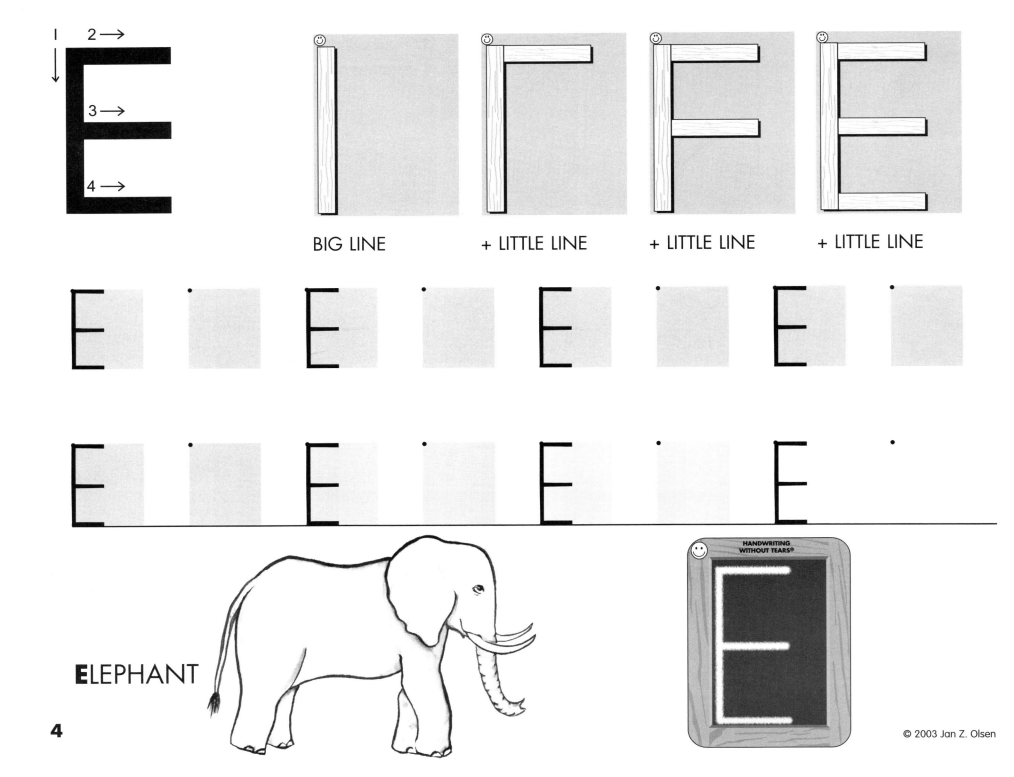

BIG LINE   + LITTLE LINE   + LITTLE LINE   + LITTLE LINE

ELEPHANT

4

© 2003 Jan Z. Olsen

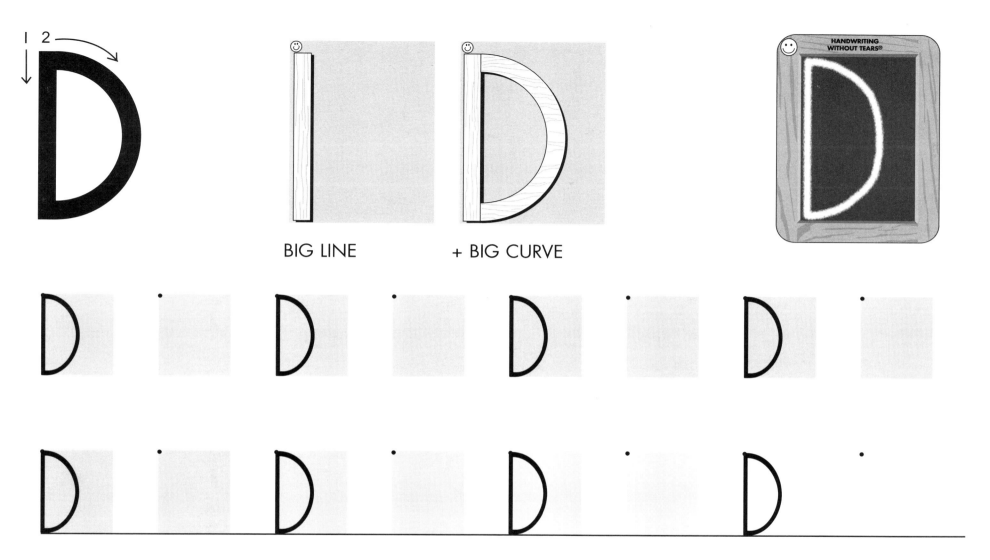

BIG LINE + BIG CURVE

DUCK

BIG LINE + LITTLE CURVE

PEAR

PIG

6

BIG LINE + LITTLE CURVE + LITTLE CURVE

BALLOONS

7

R

BIG LINE + LITTLE CURVE + LITTLE LINE

RAIN

8

© 2003 Jan Z. Olsen

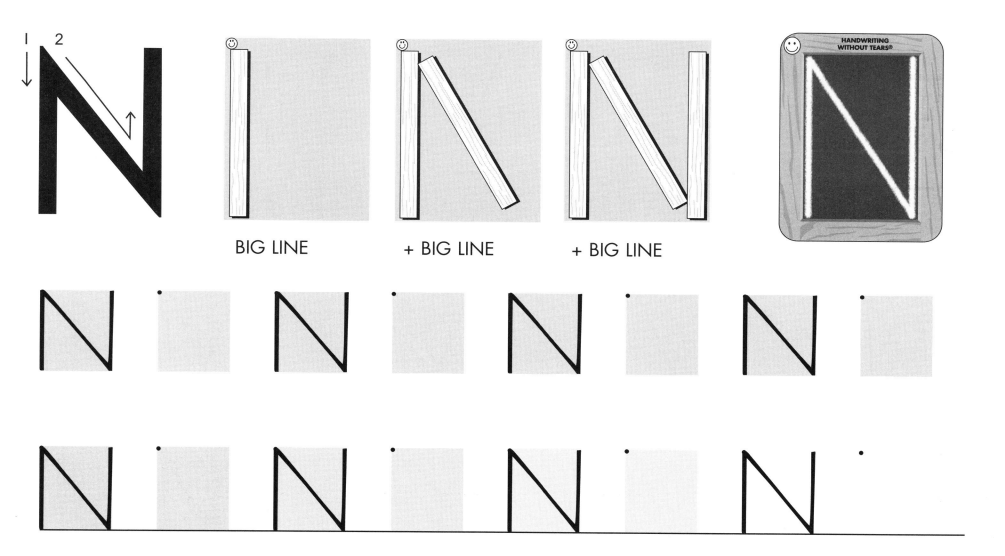

BIG LINE   + BIG LINE   + BIG LINE

NEWSPAPER

9

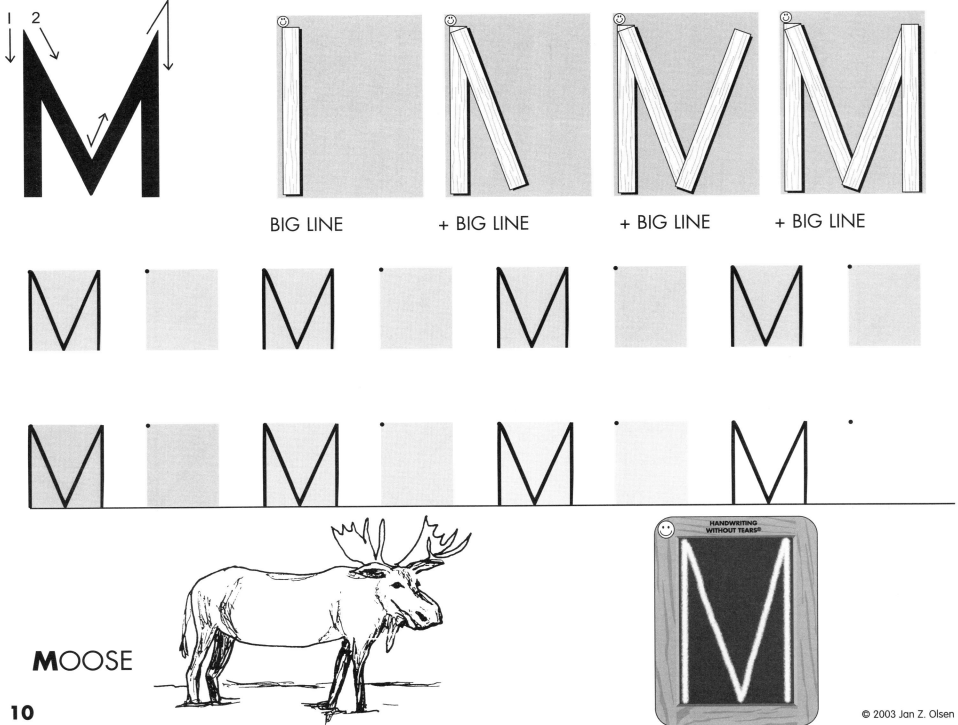

BIG LINE + BIG LINE + BIG LINE + BIG LINE

MOOSE

HANDWRITING WITHOUT TEARS®

10

© 2003 Jan Z. Olsen

FROG JUMP CAPITALS

Start in the "starting corner." Make a "big line" down. Jump back to the "starting corner" and finish the letter.

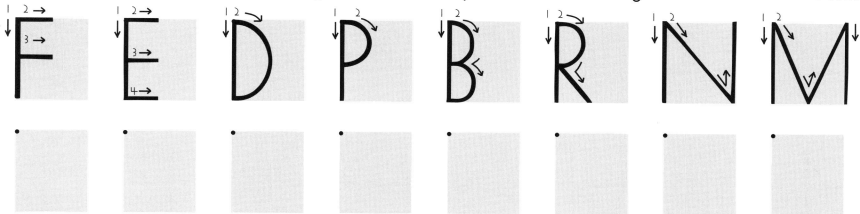

MYSTERY GAME FOR FROG JUMP CAPITALS

Start in the "starting corner." Make a "big line" down. Jump back to the "starting corner."
Wait for your teacher to tell you which Frog Jump Capital to make.

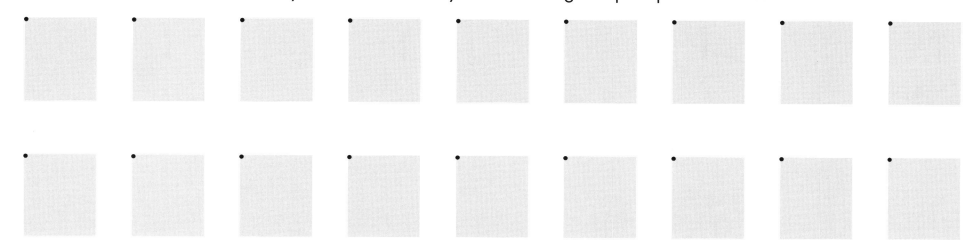

11

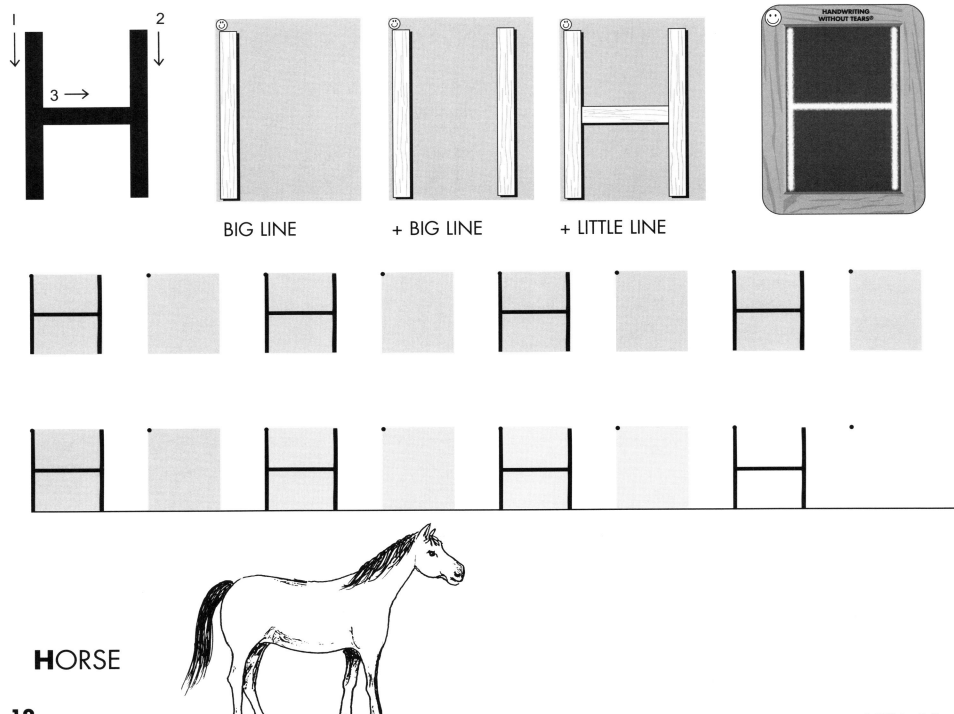

BIG LINE   + BIG LINE   + LITTLE LINE

HORSE

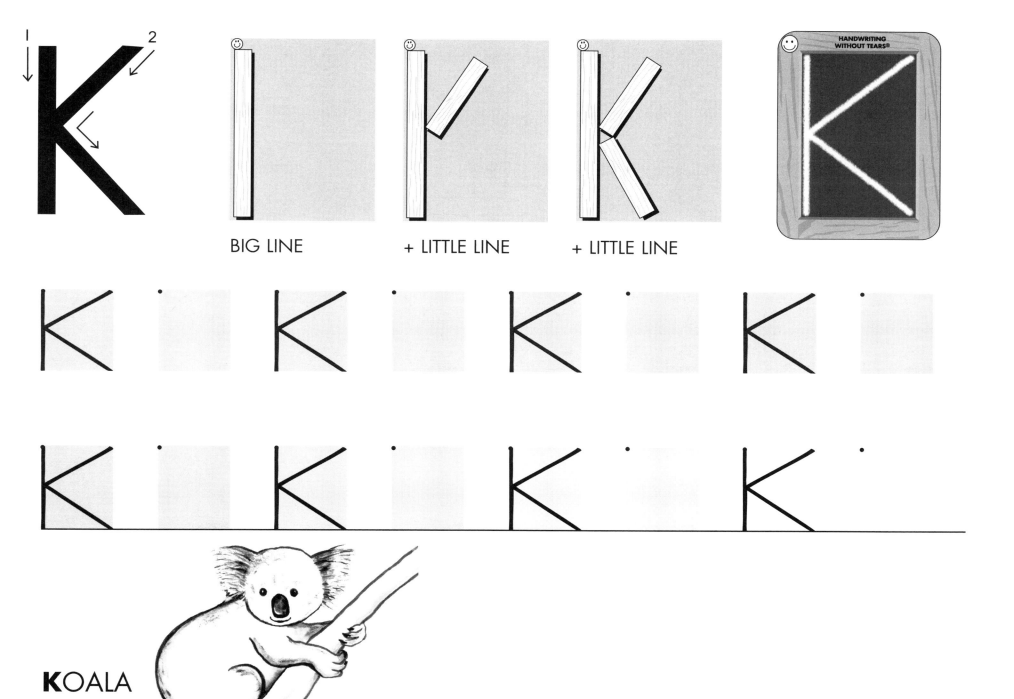

BIG LINE   + LITTLE LINE   + LITTLE LINE

KOALA

13

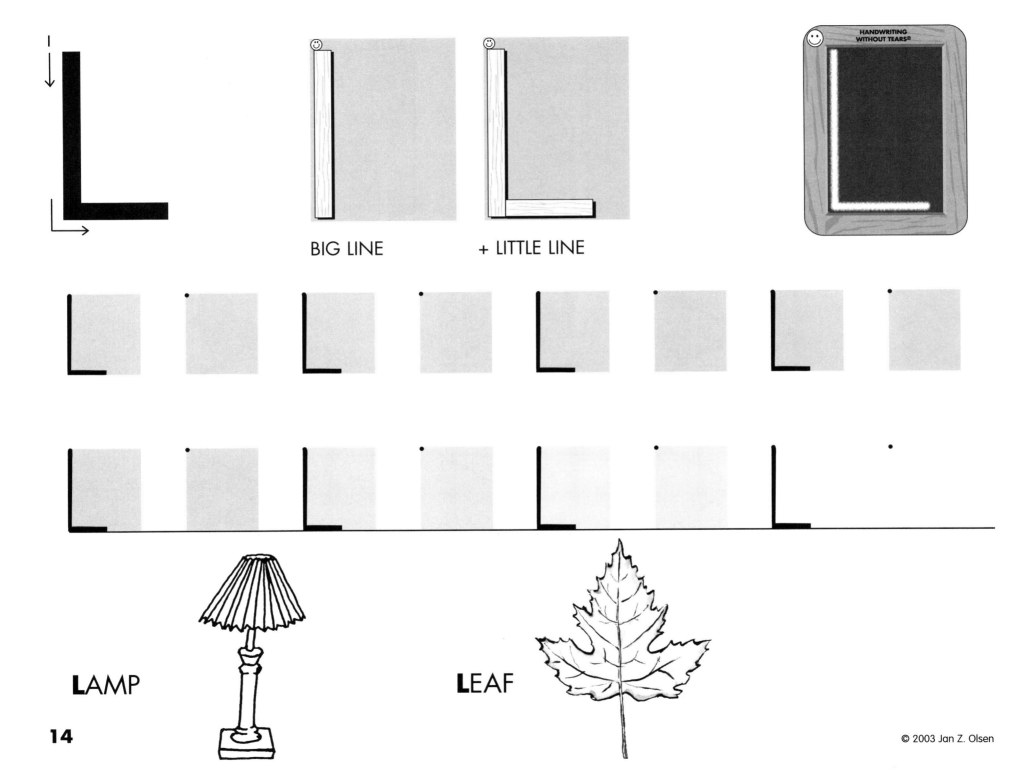

BIG LINE   + LITTLE LINE

LAMP

LEAF

14

U

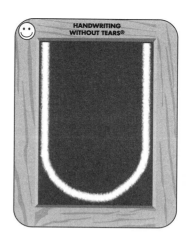

Note: We do not use HWT Wood Pieces to teach this letter.

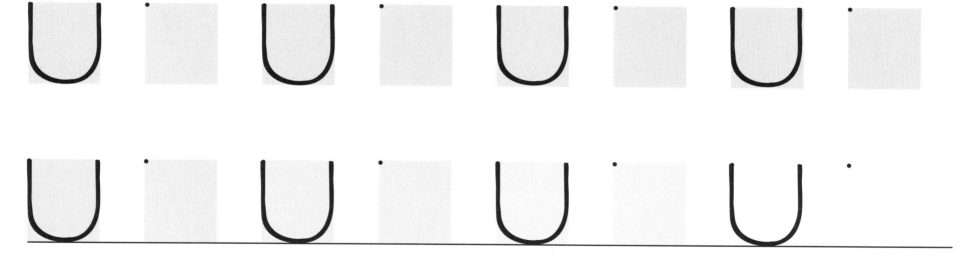

UMBRELLA

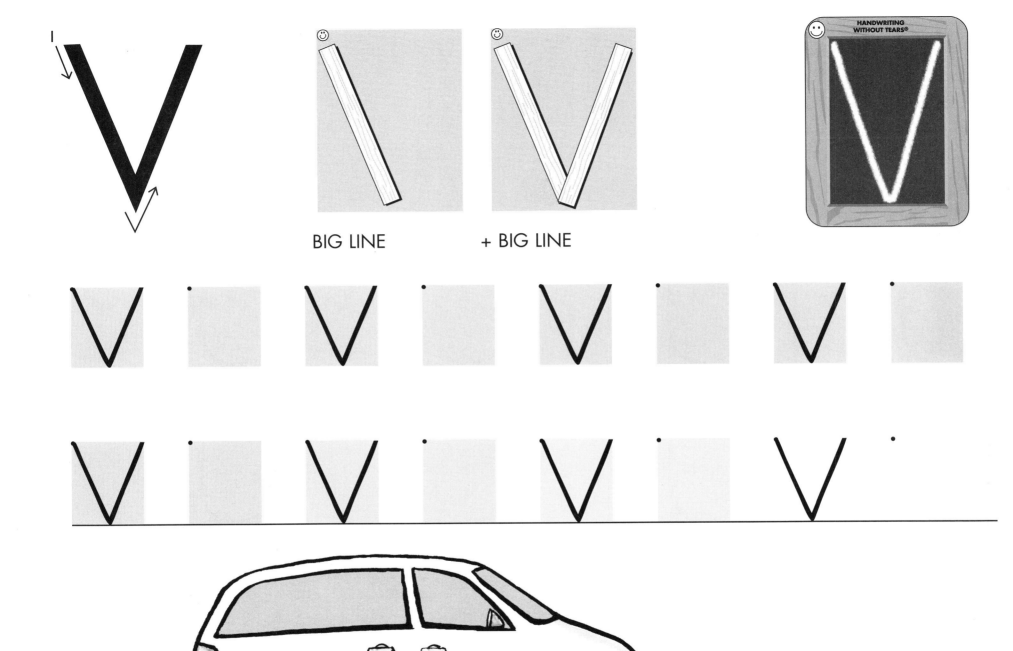

BIG LINE   + BIG LINE

VAN

16

W

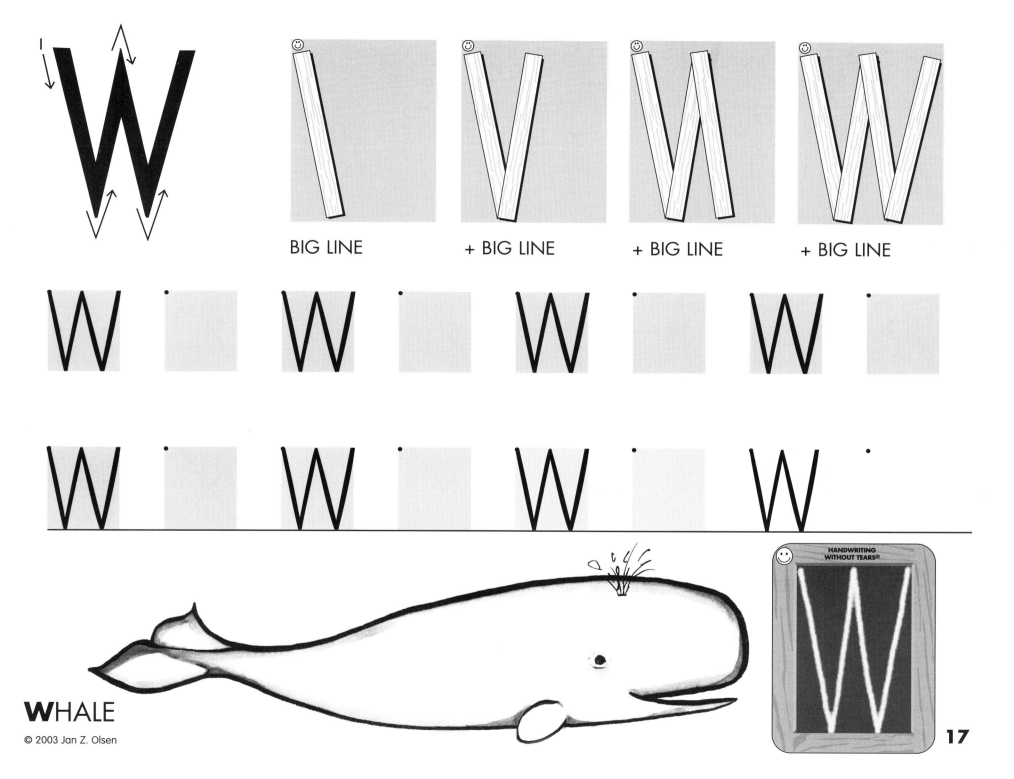

BIG LINE   + BIG LINE   + BIG LINE   + BIG LINE

WHALE

© 2003 Jan Z. Olsen

17

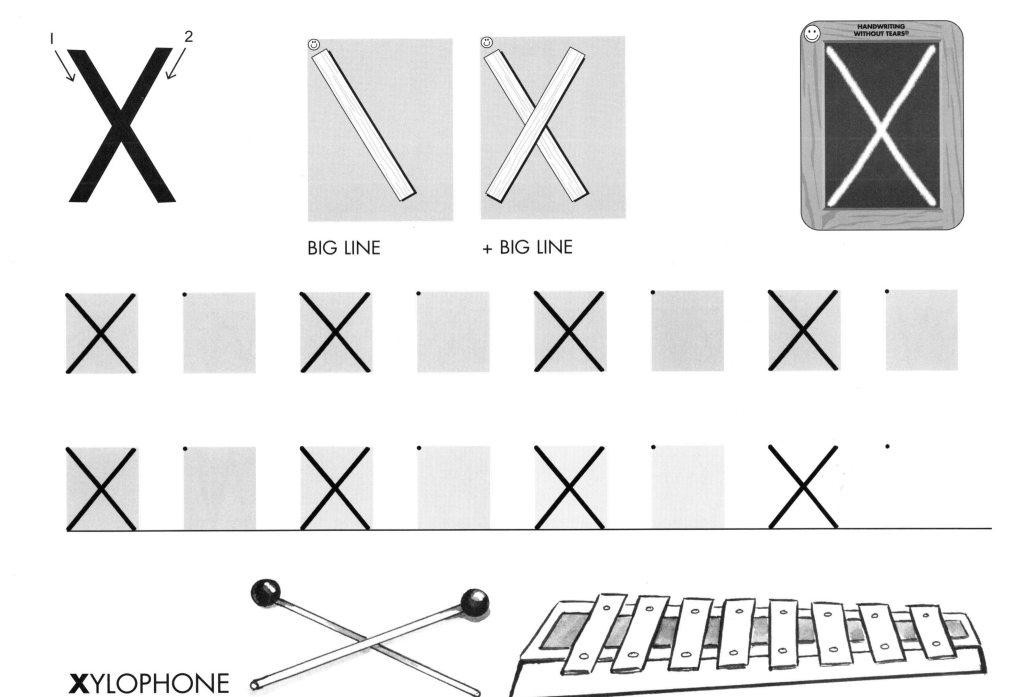

BIG LINE + BIG LINE

XYLOPHONE

18

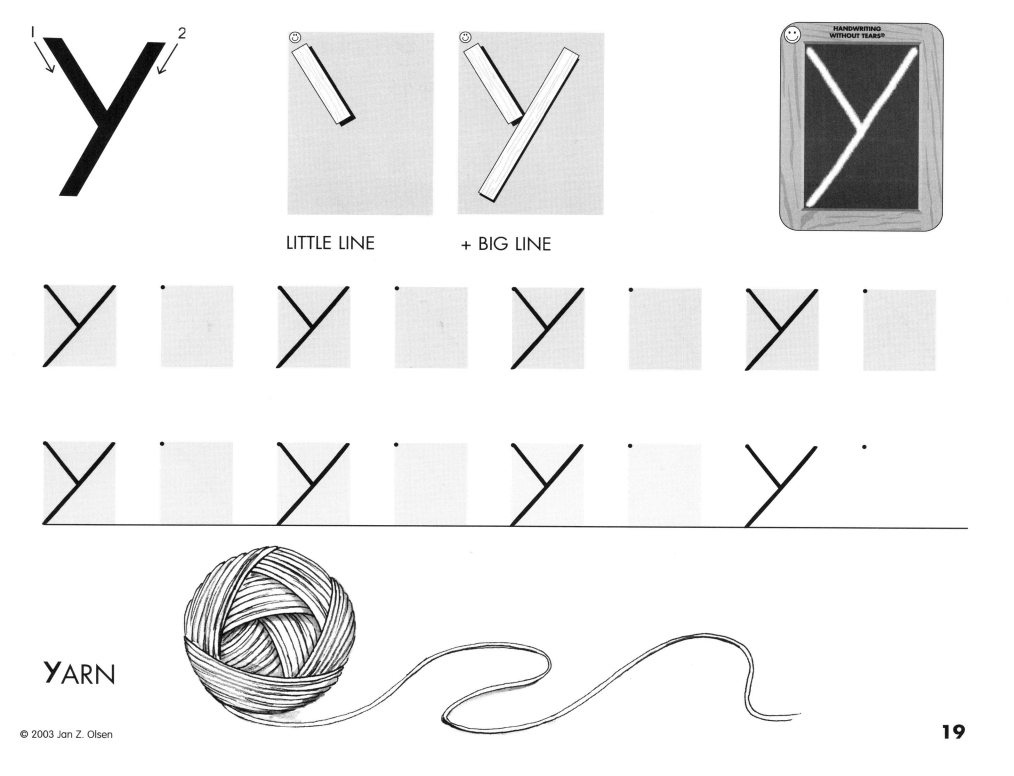

LITTLE LINE + BIG LINE

HANDWRITING WITHOUT TEARS®

YARN

19

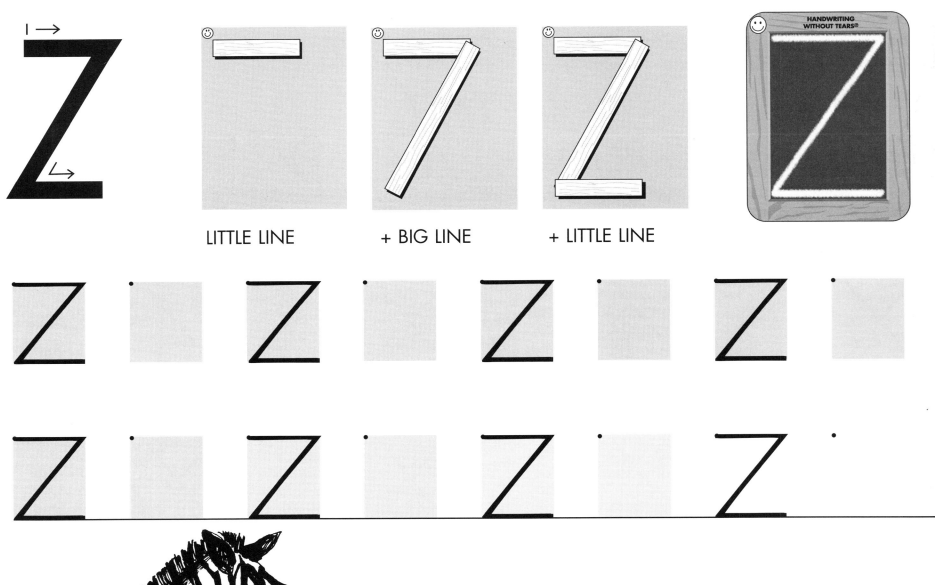

LITTLE LINE   + BIG LINE   + LITTLE LINE

ZEBRA

WORDS FOR ME

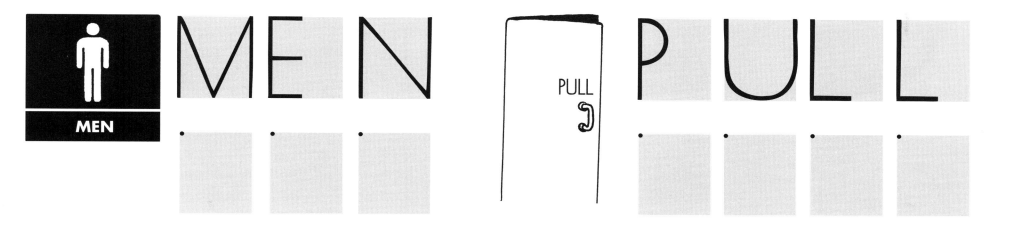

MEN

PULL

R R

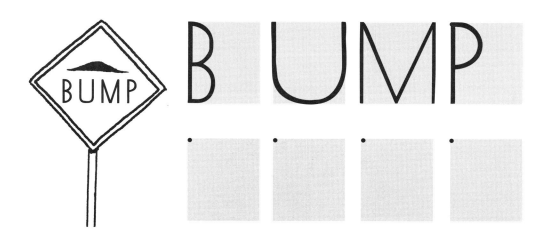

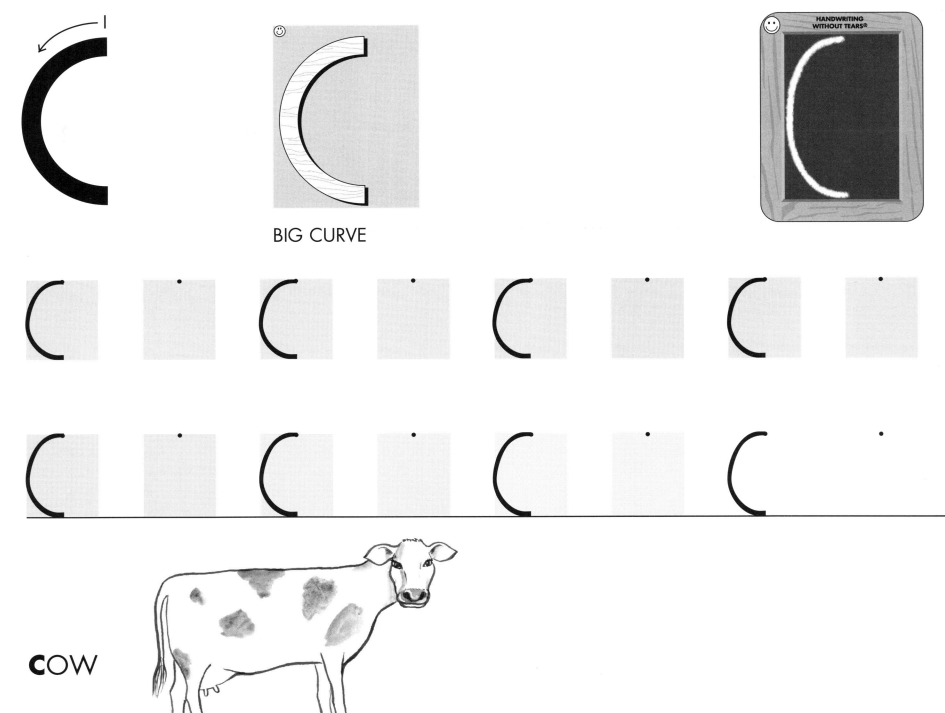

BIG CURVE

COW

22

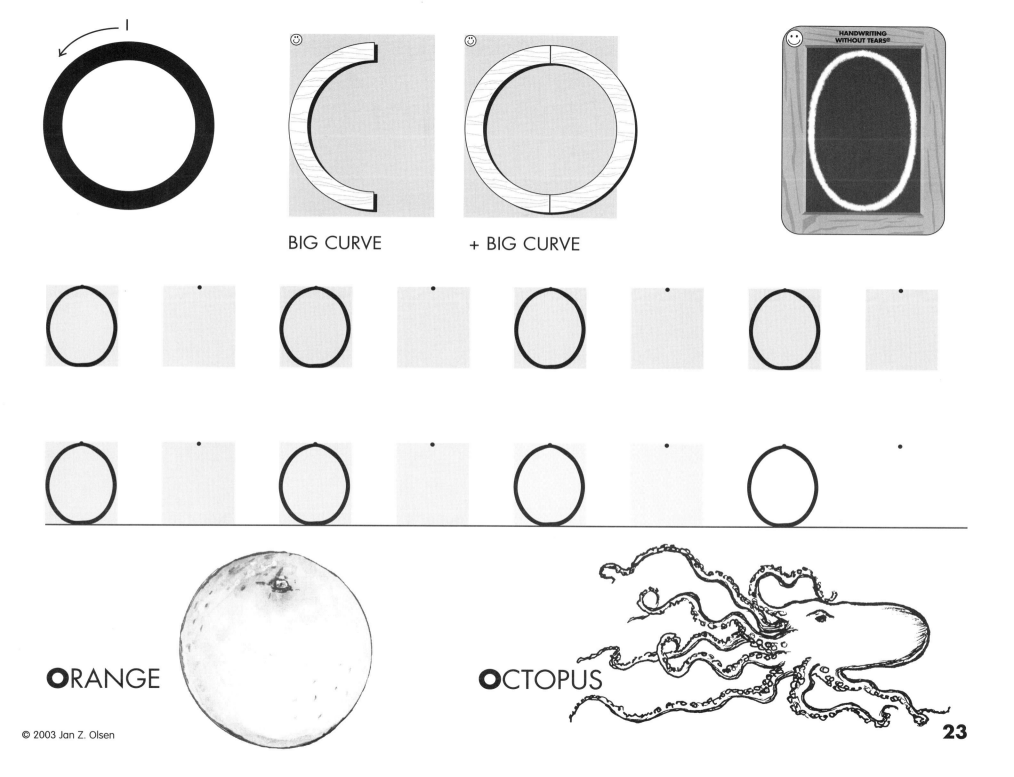

BIG CURVE + BIG CURVE

ORANGE

OCTOPUS

23

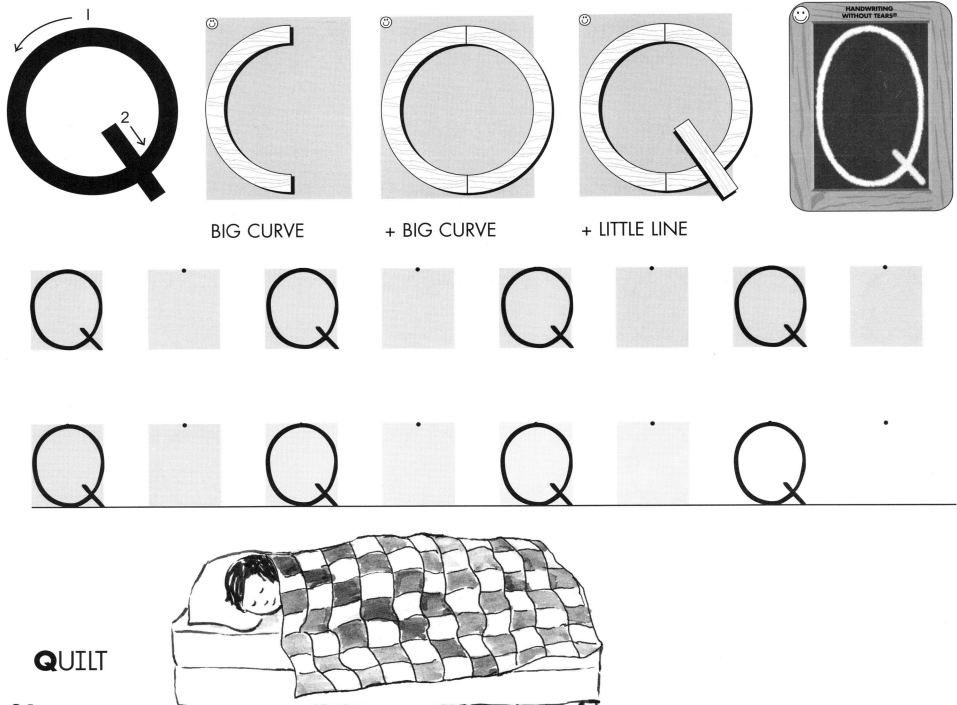

BIG CURVE   + BIG CURVE   + LITTLE LINE

QUILT

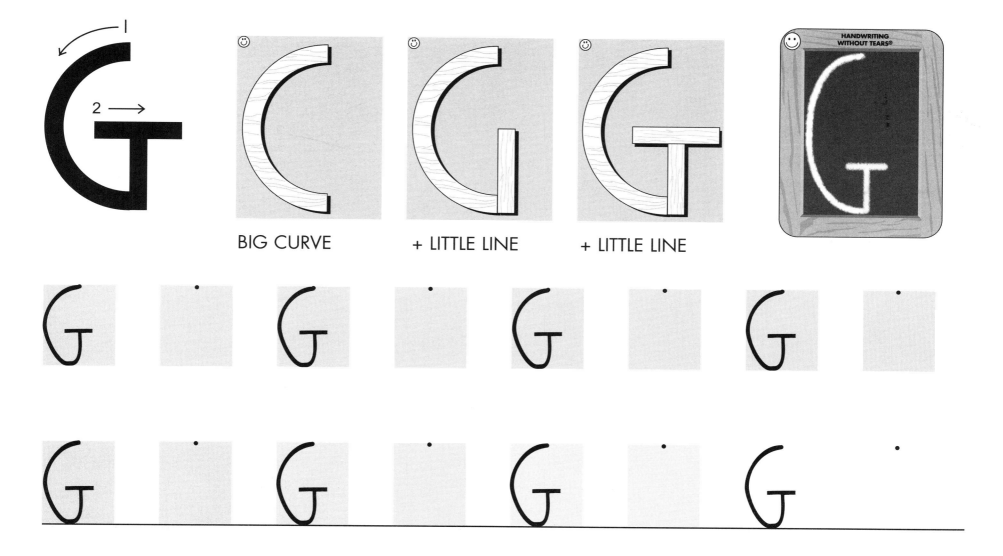

BIG CURVE   + LITTLE LINE   + LITTLE LINE

GRAPES

"MAGIC C" CAPITALS

Use a "Magic C" to make O, Q and G.

MYSTERY GAME FOR "MAGIC C" CAPITALS

Start on the dot. Make a "Magic C." Wait for your teacher to tell you which "Magic C" Capital to make.

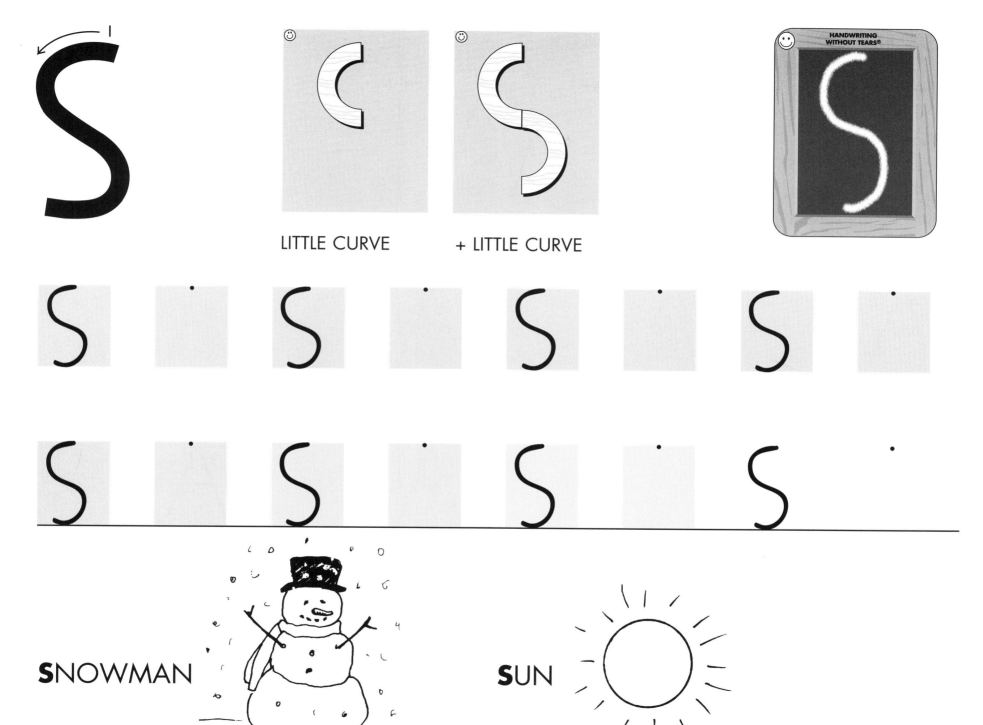

S

LITTLE CURVE   + LITTLE CURVE

SNOWMAN

SUN

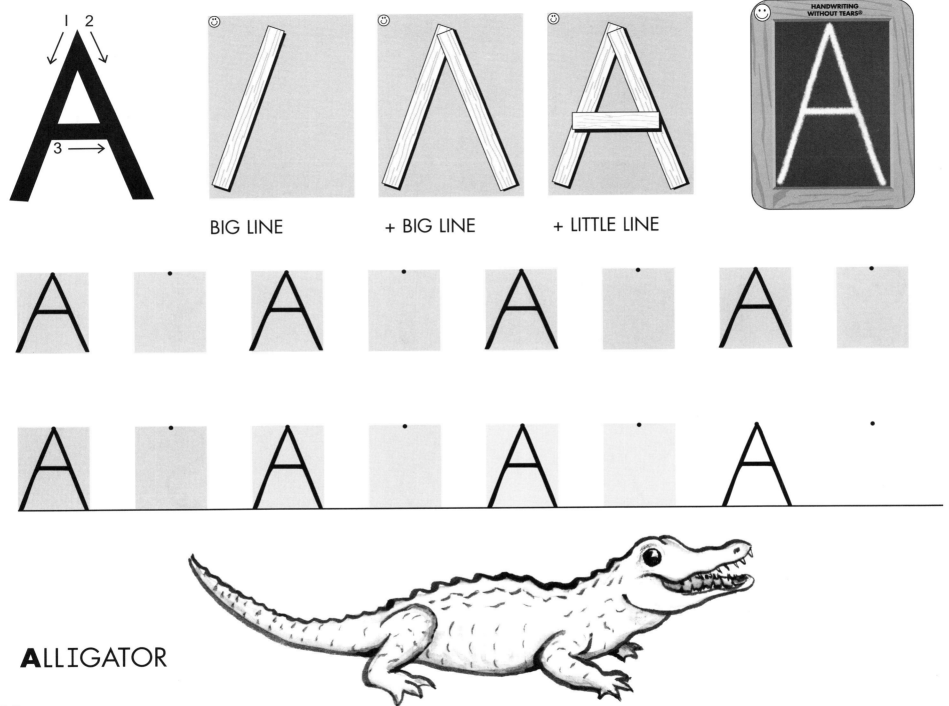

BIG LINE   + BIG LINE   + LITTLE LINE

ALLIGATOR

28

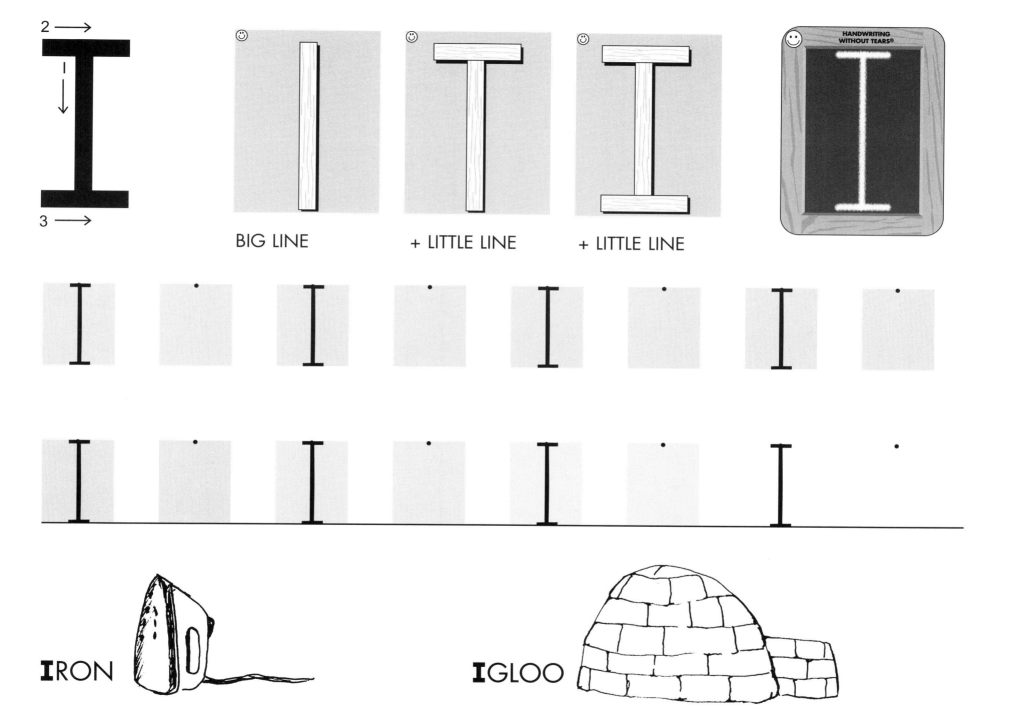

BIG LINE   + LITTLE LINE   + LITTLE LINE

IRON

IGLOO

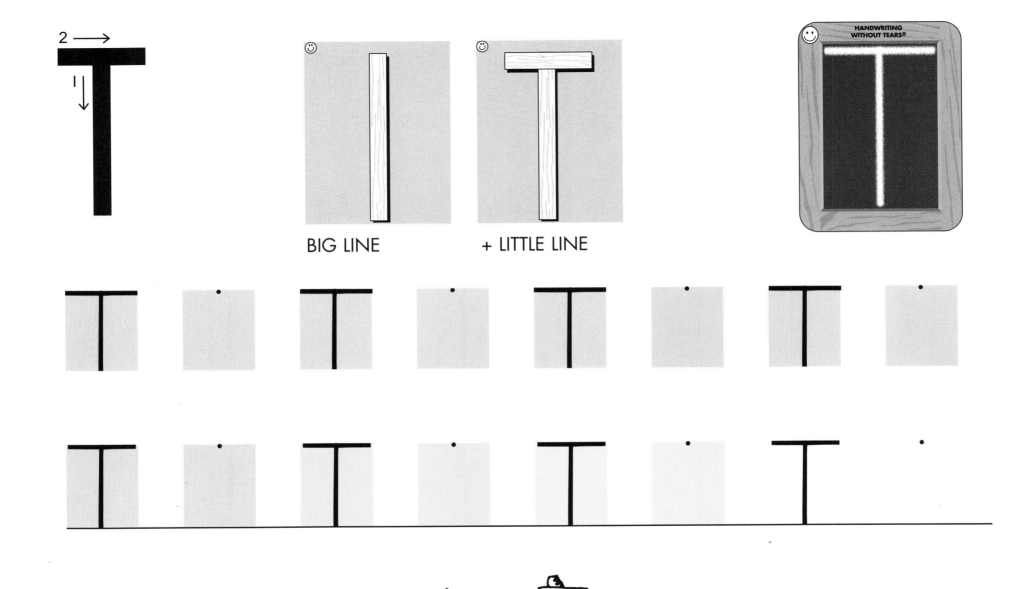

BIG LINE   + LITTLE LINE

TOW **T**RUCK

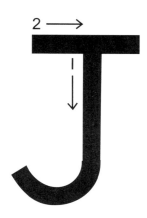

2 →

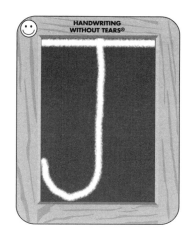

HANDWRITING WITHOUT TEARS®

Note: We do not use HWT Wood Pieces to teach this letter.

 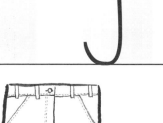 

JEANS

WORDS FOR ME

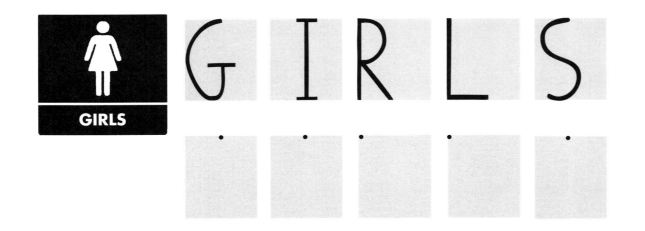

32

CAPITAL LETTERS FOR ME

A B C D E F G H I

J K L M N O P Q R

S T U V W X Y Z

33

Numbers for Me

Numbers with the HWT Slate — "Wet - Dry - Try"

Teacher's Part

Student's Part

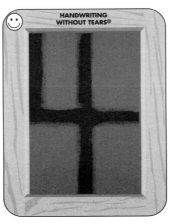

Teacher demonstrates correct number formation.

WET

Wet tiny sponge. Squeeze out. Trace the number with the sponge.
Now wet your index finger and trace the number again.

DRY

Use a small piece of paper towel to trace the number dry. Repeat 2 or 3 times.

TRY

Now, try writing the number with a small piece of chalk.

Numbers with the HWT Gray Blocks

Gray blocks are "pictures" of the slates. On the next 10 pages write numbers in the gray blocks. Follow teacher's demonstration.

        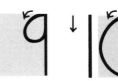

34

I starts in the starting corner!

I makes a big line down.

I stops in the corner.

one whale

☺   ☺   ☺   ☺   ☺   ☺   ☺   ☺   ☺

I can count I.

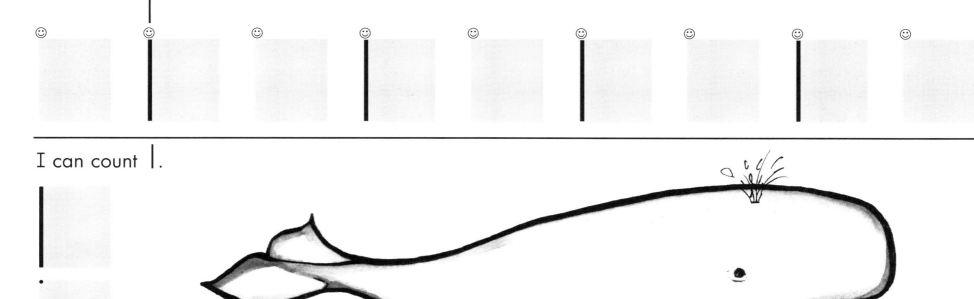

35

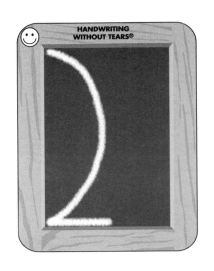

2 starts in the starting corner!
2 makes a big curve.
2 stops in the corner.
2 walks away on the bottom.

two alligators

I can write 2.

I can count to 2.

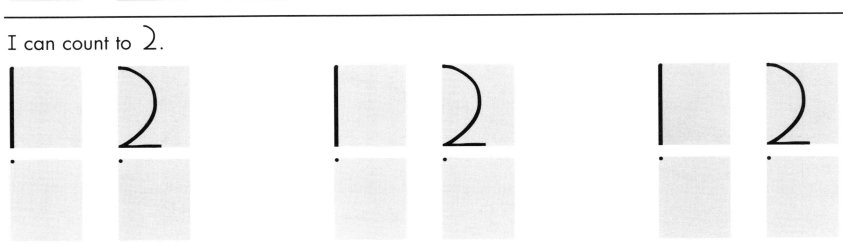

3 starts in the starting corner!

3 makes a little curve to the middle.

3 makes another little curve to the bottom corner.

three fish

I can write 3.

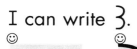

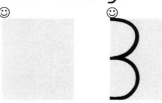   

I can count to 3.

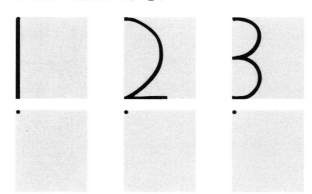

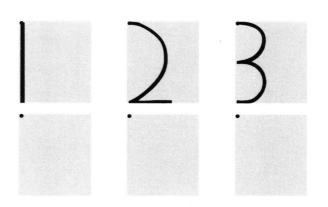

4 starts in the starting corner!
4 makes a little line down to the middle.
4 walks across the dark night!
4 jumps to the top and says, "I did it!"

four snowmen

I can write 4.

I can count to 4.

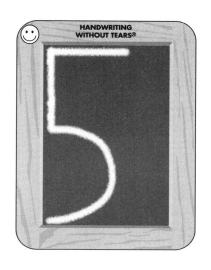

5 starts in the starting corner!

5 makes a little line down to the middle. It starts to rain.

5 turns around and goes back for an umbrella.

five umbrellas

I can write 5.

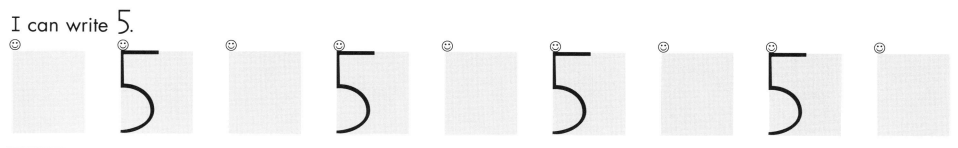

I can count to 5.

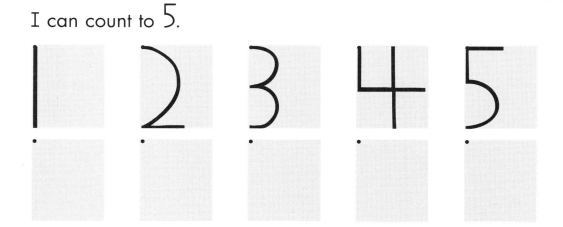

39

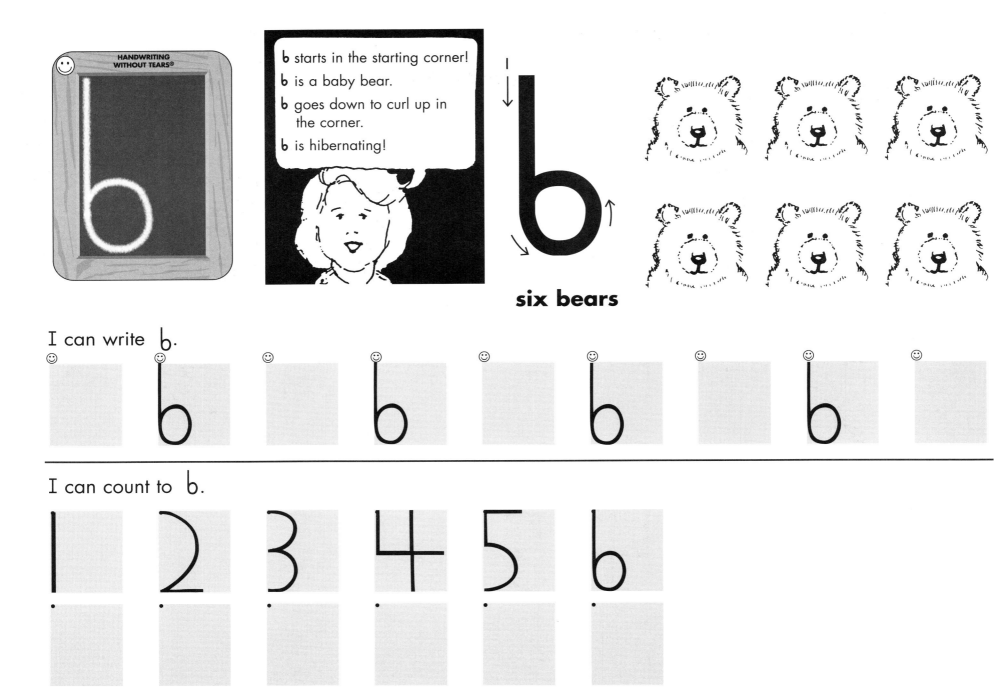

b starts in the starting corner!

b is a baby bear.

b goes down to curl up in the corner.

b is hibernating!

six bears

I can write b.

I can count to b.

40

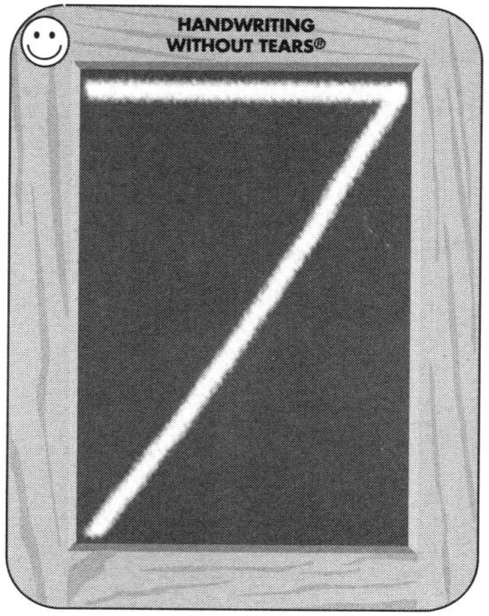

7 starts in the starting corner!

7 is on the top.

7 walks across the top!

7 says, "I better slide down."

I →

seven lamps

I can write 7.

I can count to 7.

1 2 3 4 5 6 7

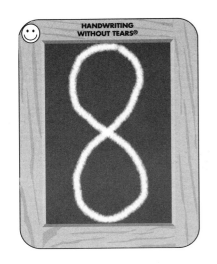

HANDWRITING WITHOUT TEARS®

8 is different!

8 doesn't like corners.

8 starts in the center.

8 begins with S and then says, "I want to go home."

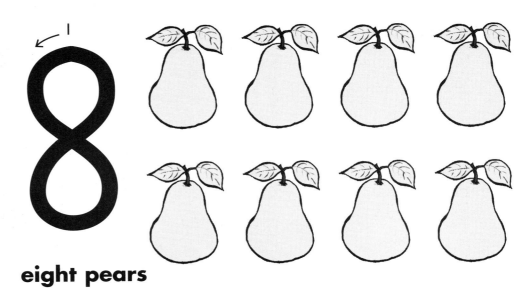

eight pears

I can write 8.

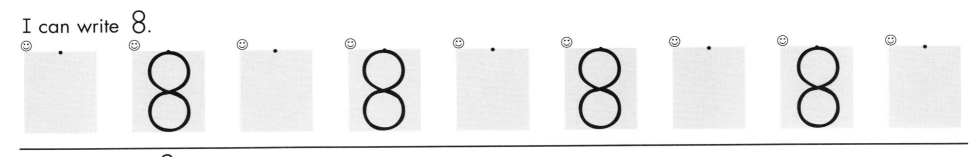

I can count to 8.

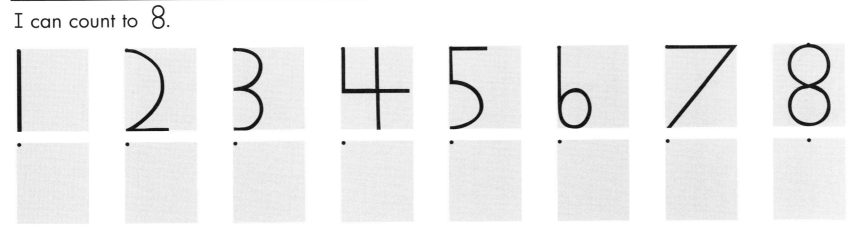

9 is so special!

9 has its own corner.

9 makes a little curve.

9 goes up to the corner.

9 makes a big line down.

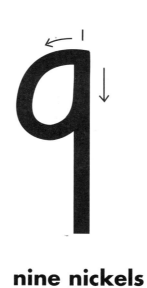

nine nickels

I can write 9.

I can count to 9.

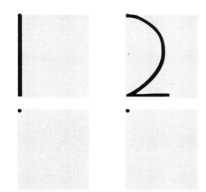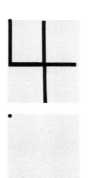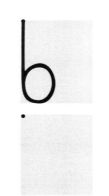

43

10 uses two places.
1 comes first.
O is next.
O starts at the top.
10 is finished!

ten balloons

I can write 10.

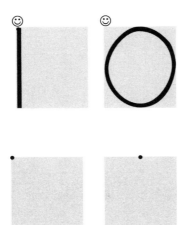
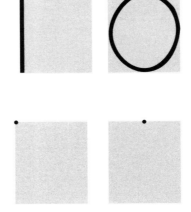
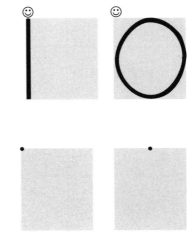

Numbers for Me

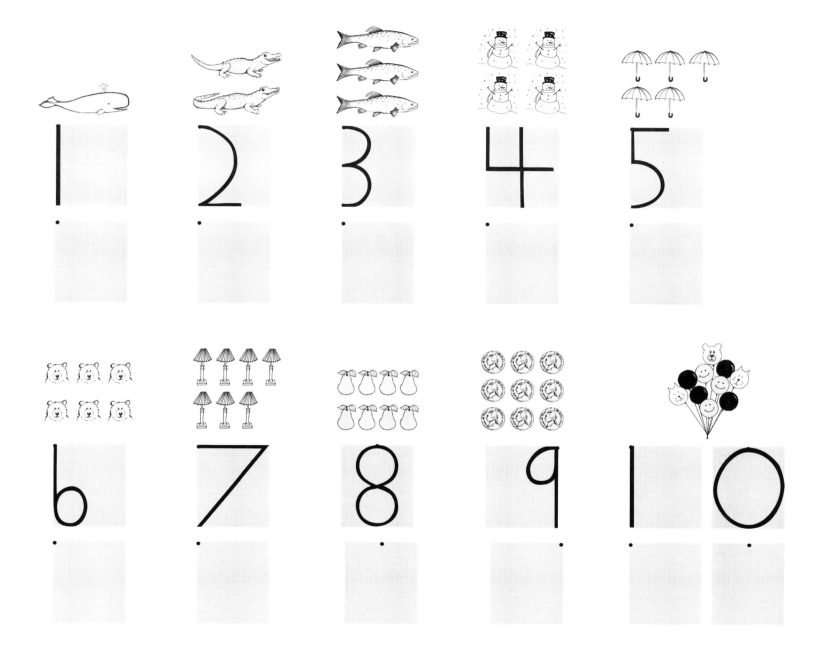

Lowercase Letters for Me

Lowercase Letters are Fun!

Your children are ready for lowercase printing. The focus will be on letter formation and placing letters correctly on the lines. You may alter the order of teaching to meet the needs of your child or class.

Capital Partners

These lowercase letters have the same formation as the capitals.

c   o   s   v   w

Lowercase t is similar to capital T. It is just crossed lower.

t

"Magic c" Letters

"Magic c" lowercase letters begin with a "c" stroke.

a   d   g

More Vowels

u   i   e

Transition Group

l   k   y   j

Diver Letters

"Diver Letters" dive down, come back up and swim over.

p   r   n   m   h   b

Final Group

Letter f has a unique starting point and can be difficult to form. Letter q begins with a "Magic c," but is introduced here to avoid confusion with g. Letters x and z use the same formation for capitals and lowercase. They are introduced at the end because they are used infrequently.

f   q   x   z

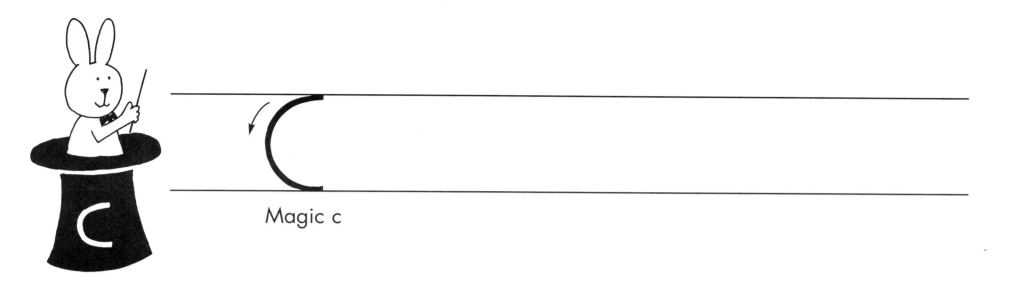

Magic c

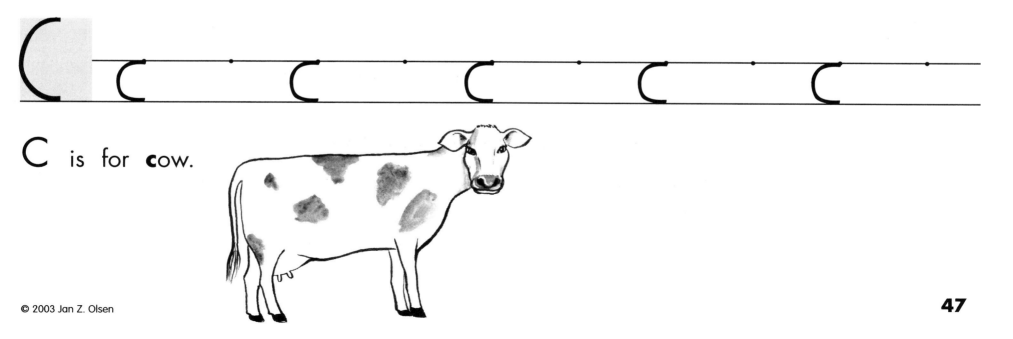

C is for cow.

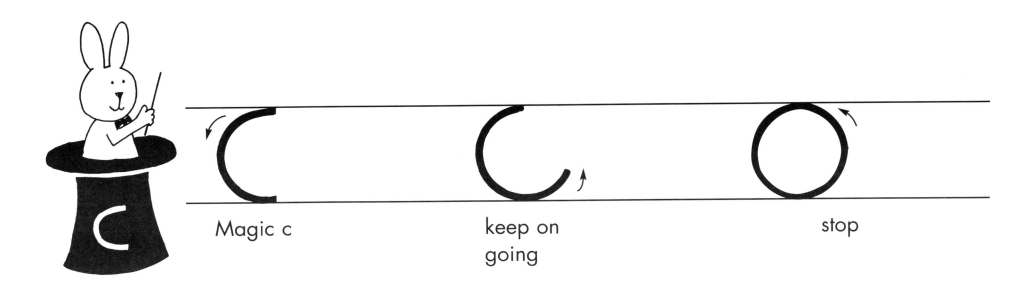

Magic c

keep on
going

stop

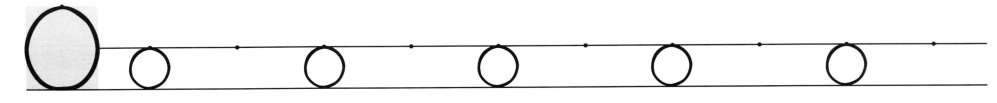

O is for **o**wl.

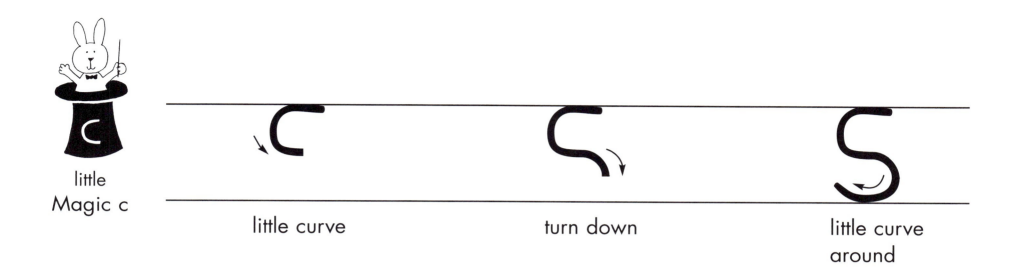

little
Magic c

little curve   turn down   little curve
around

S is for **s**nowman.

49

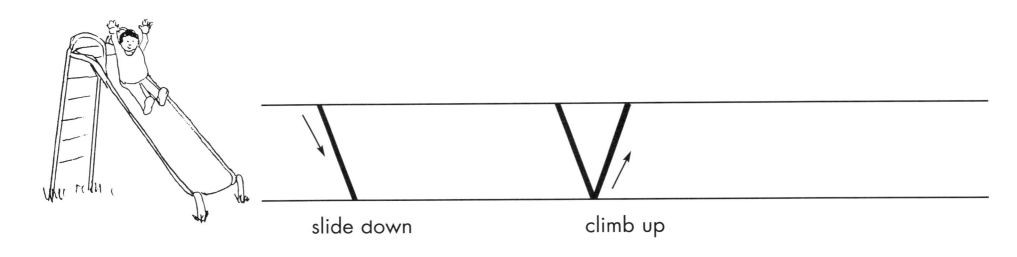

slide down   climb up

V is for **v**an.

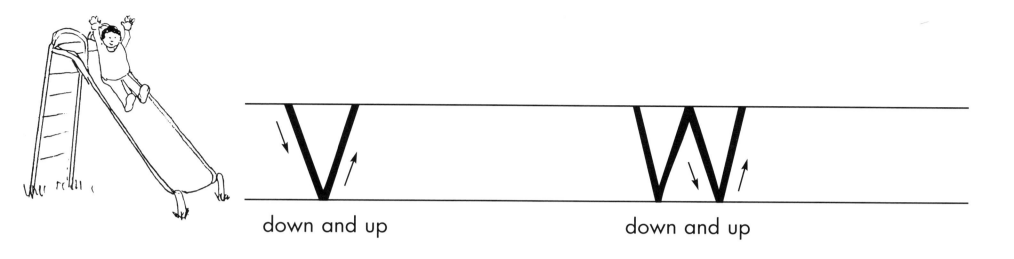

down and up   down and up

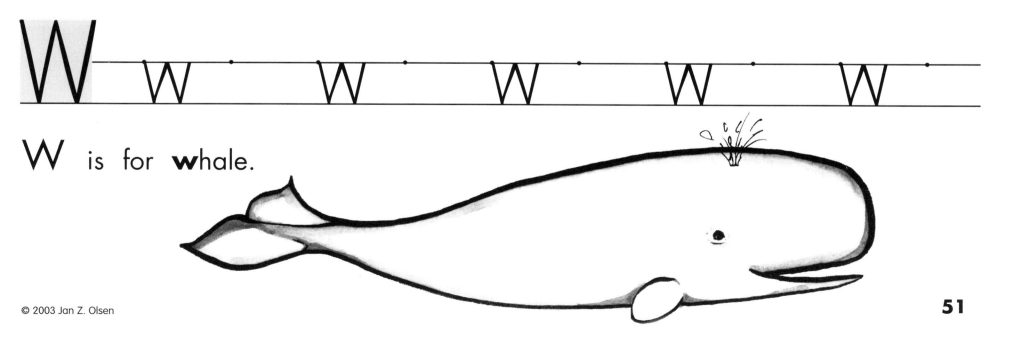

W is for **w**hale.

51

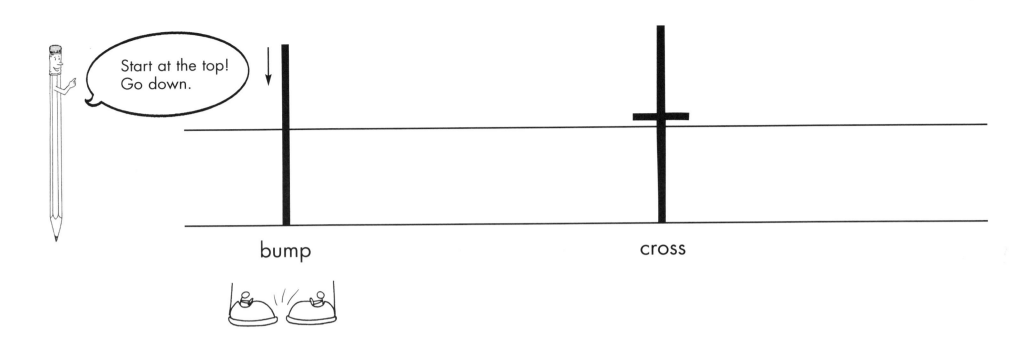

Start at the top!
Go down.

bump

cross

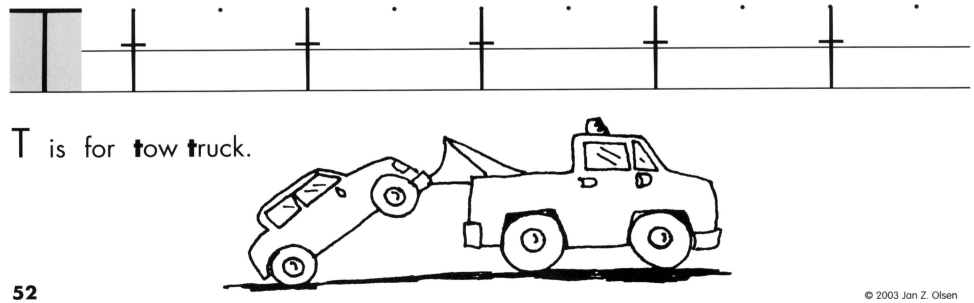

T is for **t**ow **t**ruck.

Words for Me

COW COW

WOW WOW

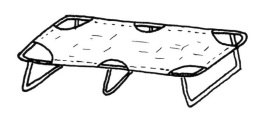

COT COT

tot tot

bump

Magic c

up like a

slide down
bump

A a a a a a

A is for **a**lligator.

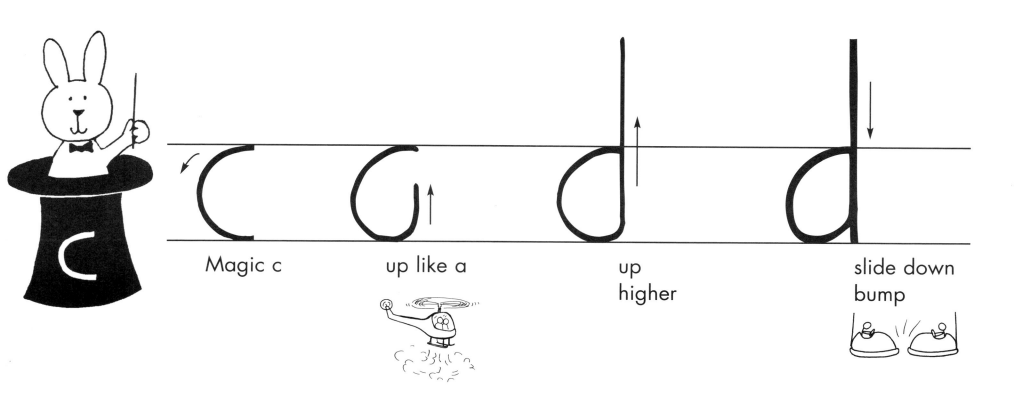

Magic c   up like a   up
higher   slide down
bump

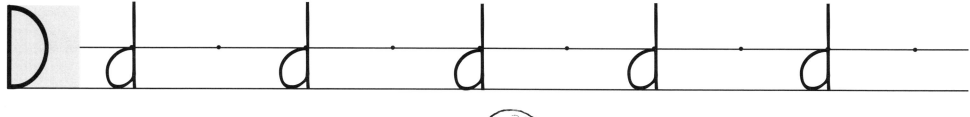

D is for **d**uck.

55

Magic c

bump

up like a

back down

turn

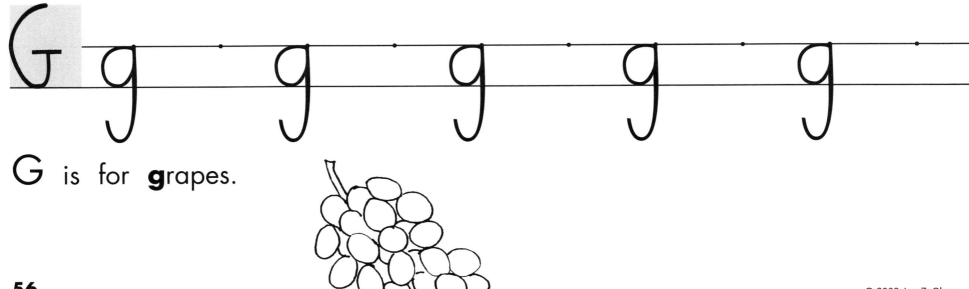

G is for **g**rapes.

Mystery Game for "Magic c" Letters

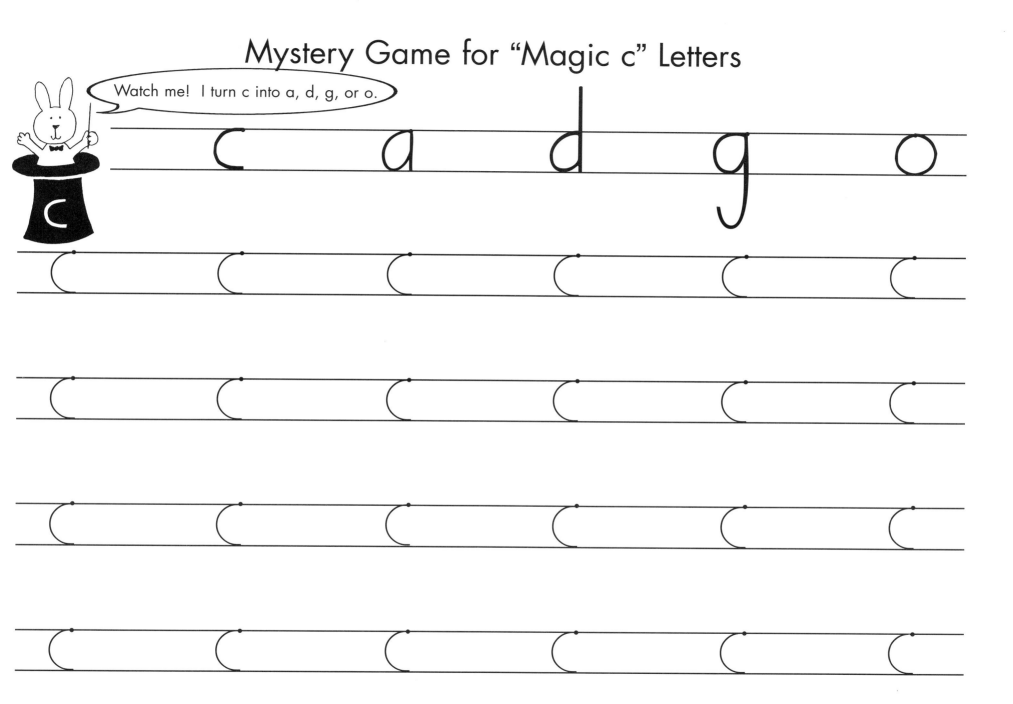

Watch me! I turn c into a, d, g, or o.

c   a   d   g   o

Tell your students to: 1. Start on the dot. 2. Trace the **c** and wait at the bottom. 3. Change **c** into a new letter. (Teacher calls out a, d, g, or o in random order.) 4. Do one line a day. **57**

Words for Me

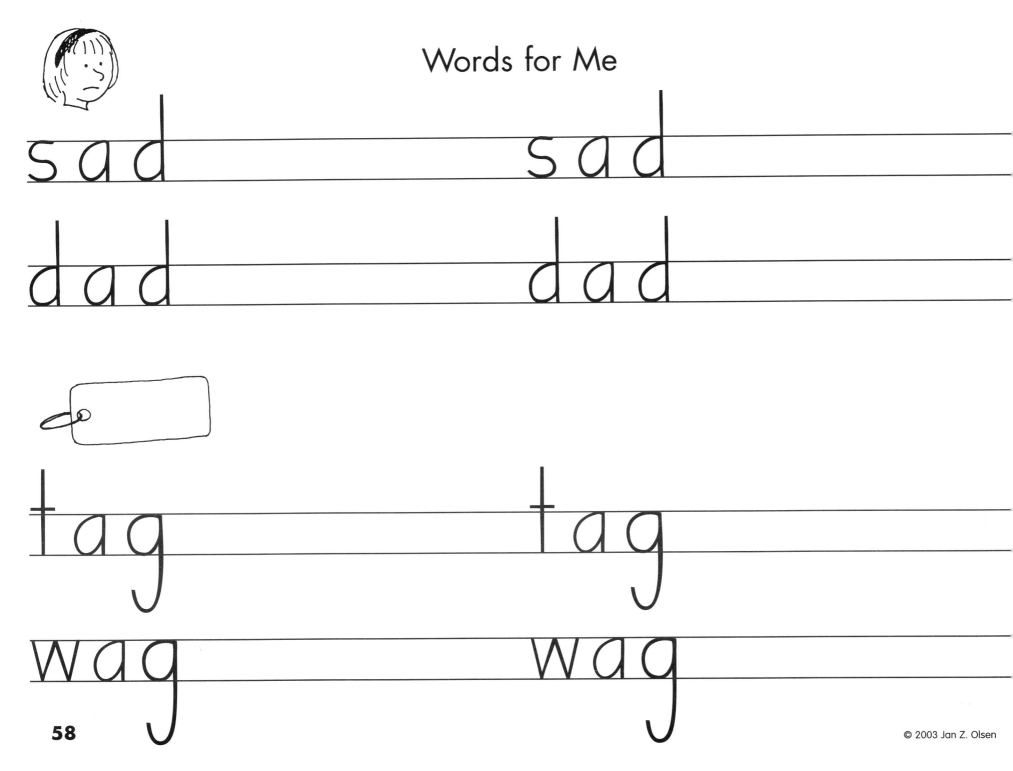

sad sad

dad dad

tag tag

wag wag

58

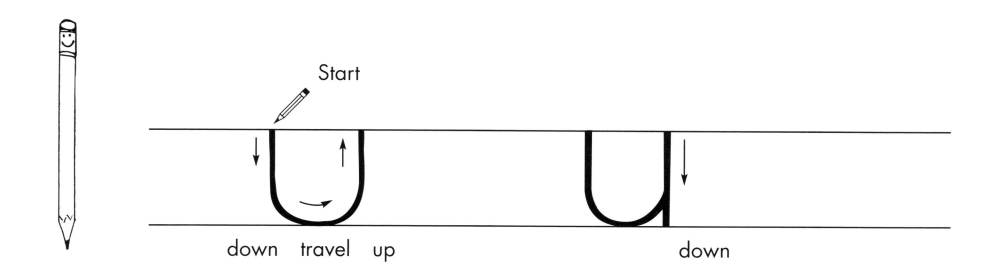

Start

down   travel   up   down

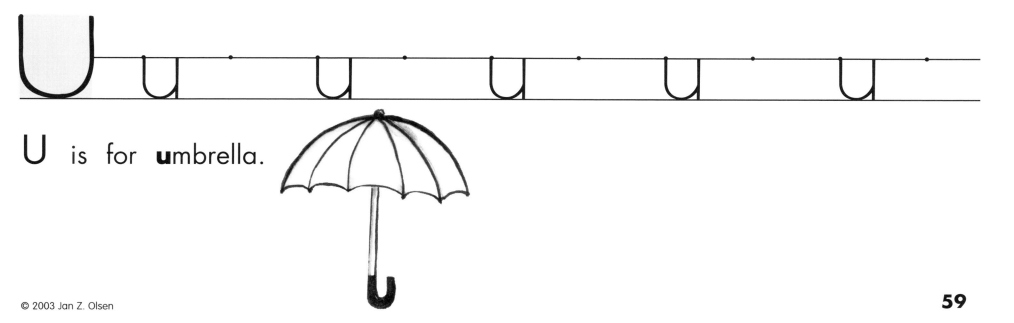

U is for **u**mbrella.

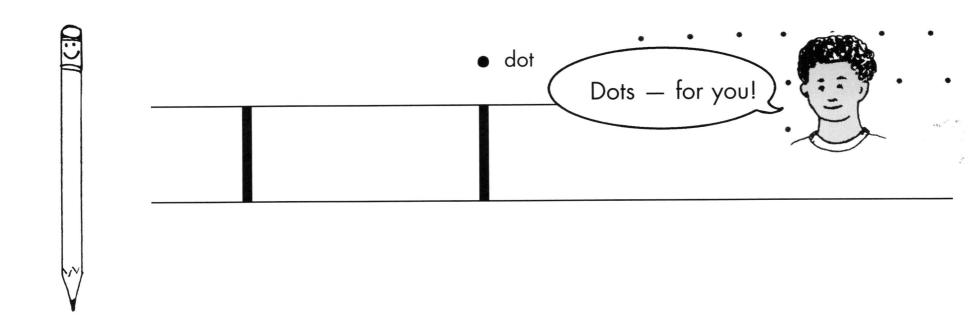

● dot

Dots — for you!

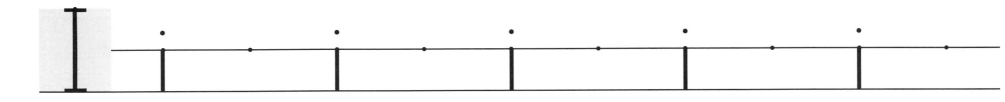

I is for **i**gloo.

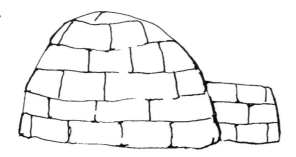

60

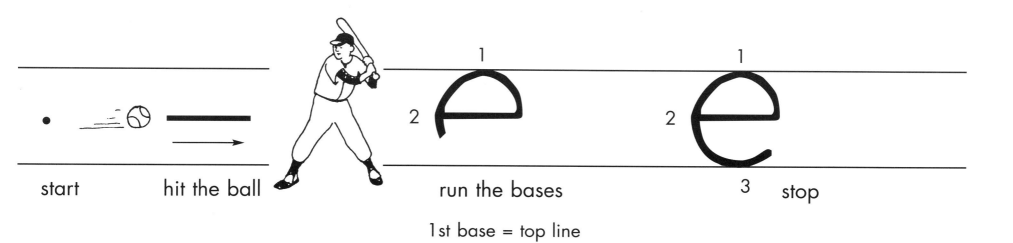

start   hit the ball   run the bases   stop

1st base = top line
2nd base = start of e
3rd base = bottom line

E e · e · e · e · e ·

E is for **e**lephant.

61

Words for Me

dice dice

ice ice

tug tug

dug dug

Sentences for Me

He   is   wet.

We   go   out.

Extra large spaces are used for beginners.

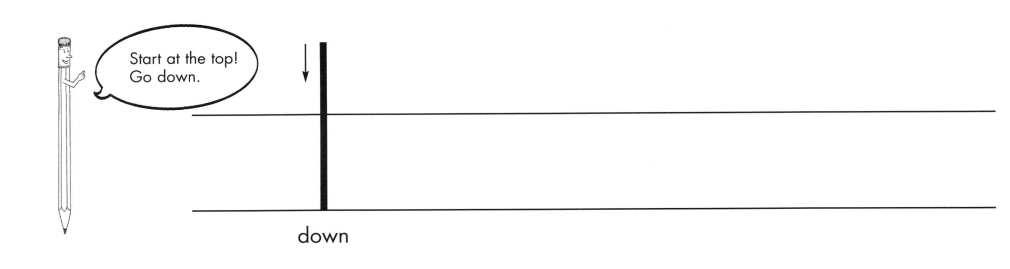

down

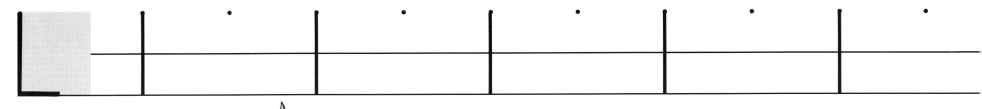

L is for leaf.

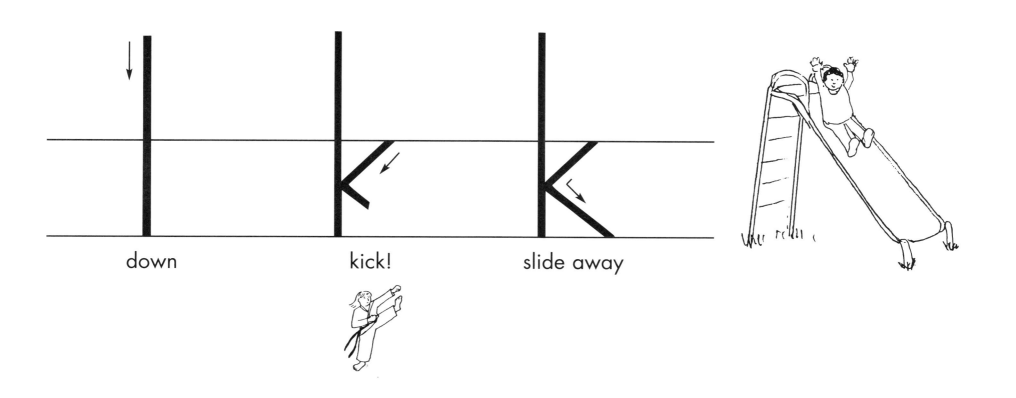

down   kick!   slide away

K is for **k**oala.

65

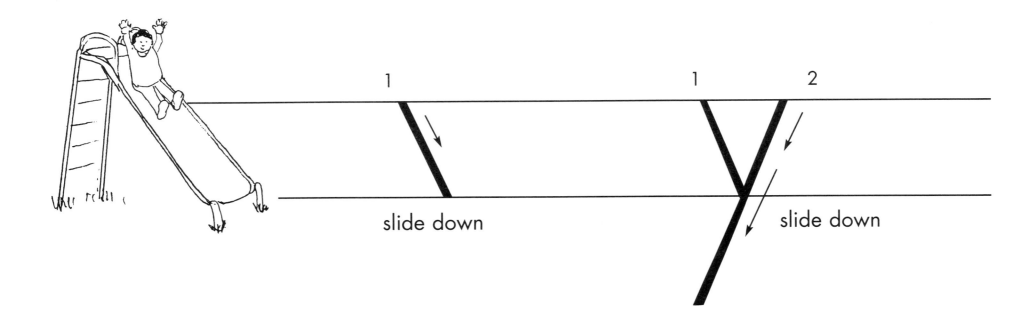

1   slide down

1 2   slide down

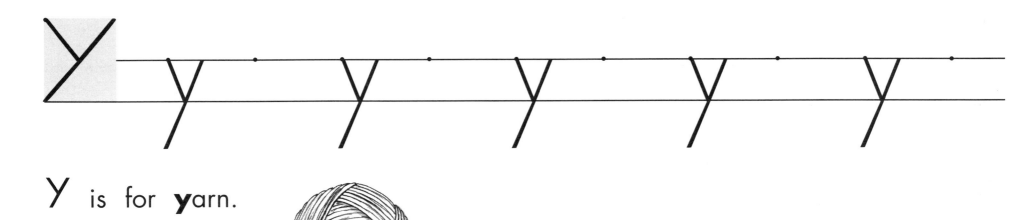

Y is for **y**arn.

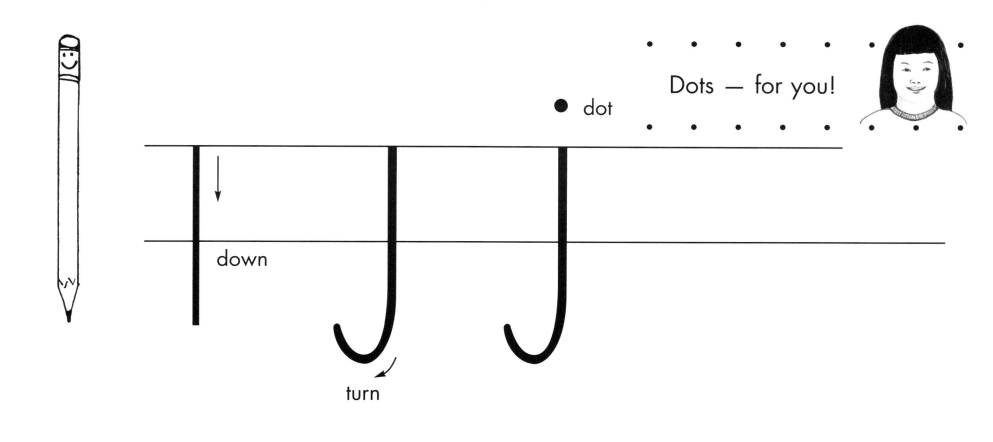

dot ● dot

Dots — for you!

down ↓

turn

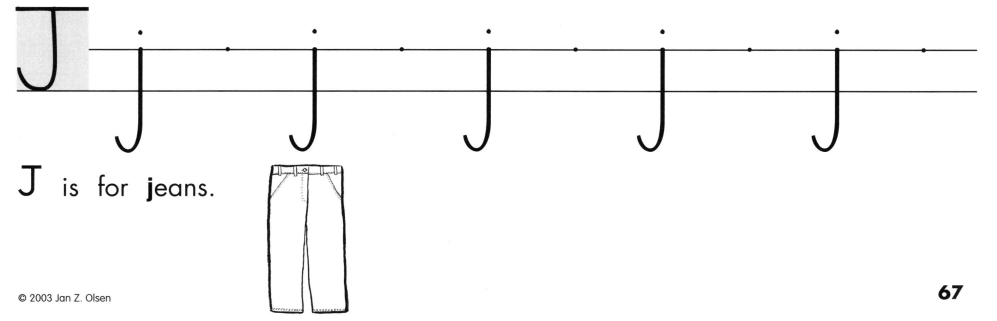

J

J is for **j**eans.

jet   jet

yet   yet

look   look

cook   cook

I like tacos.

We see you.

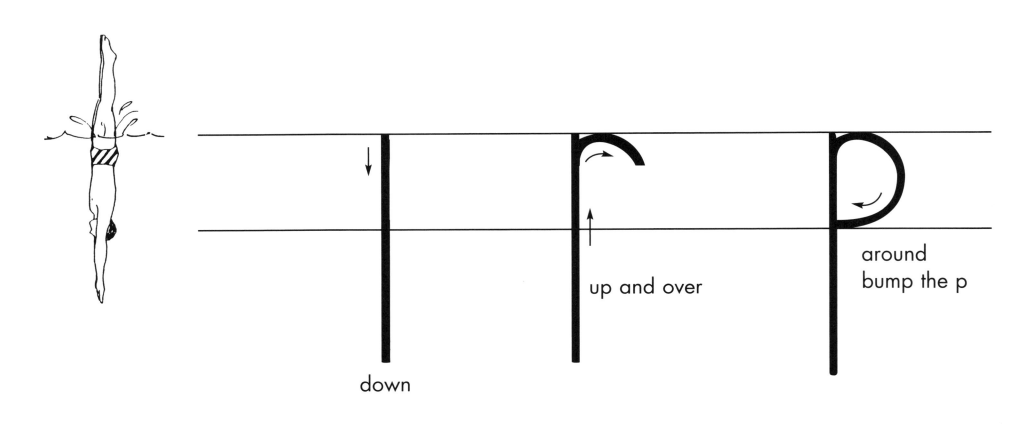

down

up and over

around
bump the p

P is for **p**enguin.

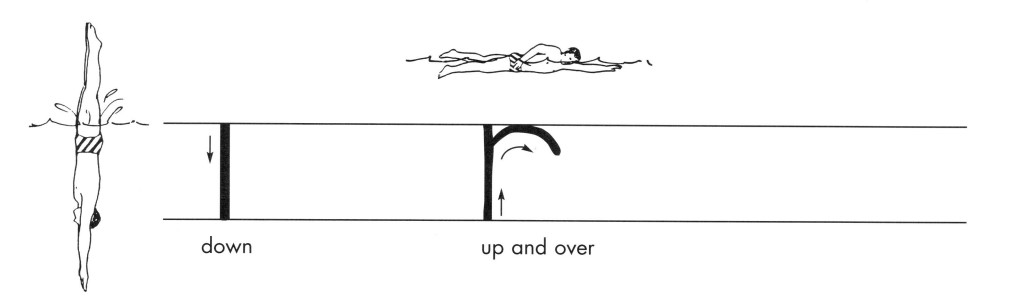

down · · · · · up and over

R r   r   r   r   r   r

R is for **r**ain.

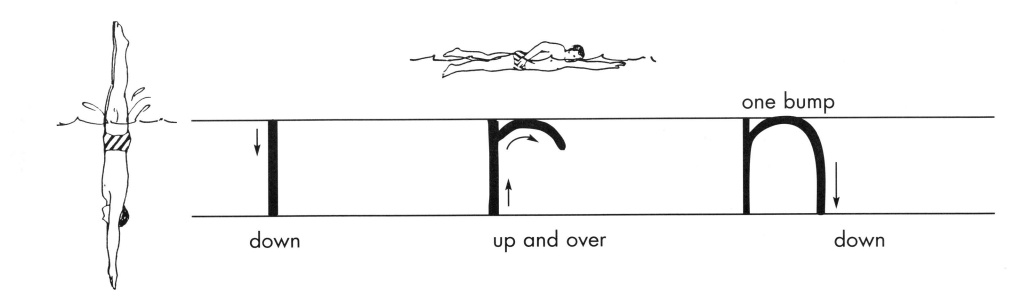

down   up and over   one bump   down

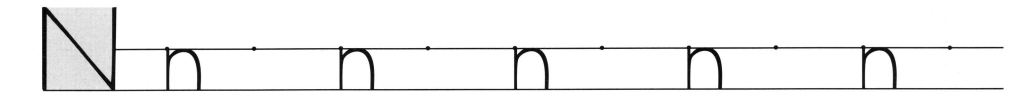

N is for **n**ewspaper.

NEWSPAPER

72

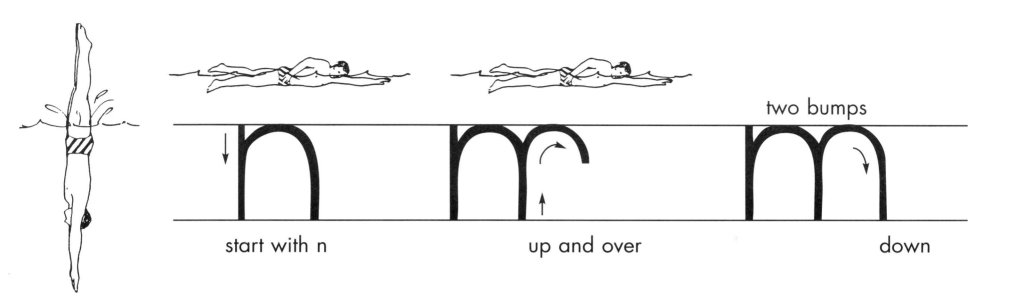

two bumps

n

m

m

start with n

up and over

down

M m m m m m

M is for **m**oose.

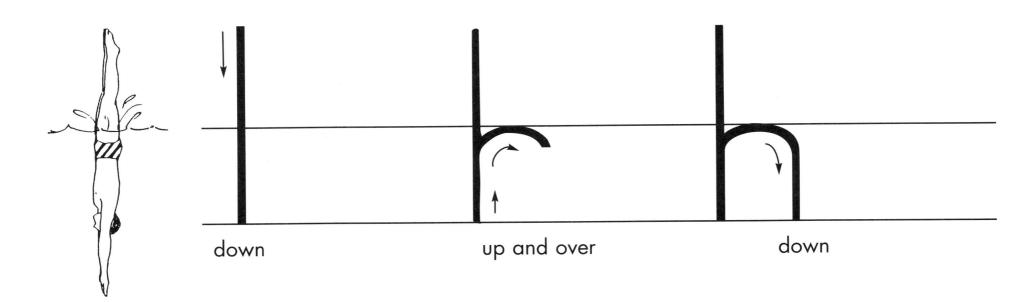

down   up and over   down

H is for **h**orse.

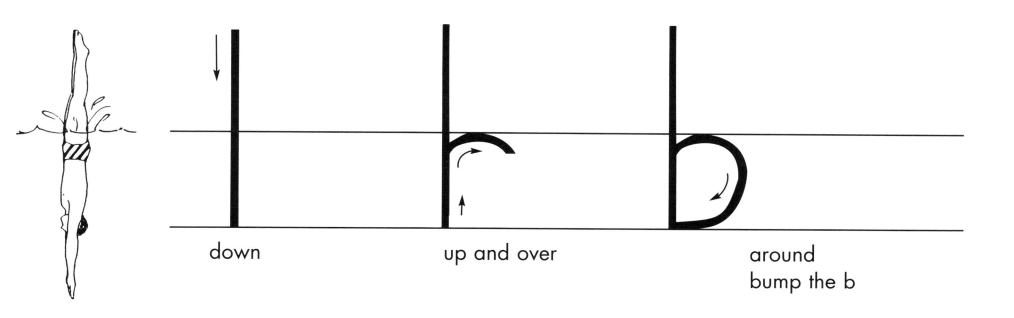

down   up and over   around
bump the b

B is for **b**alloons.

75

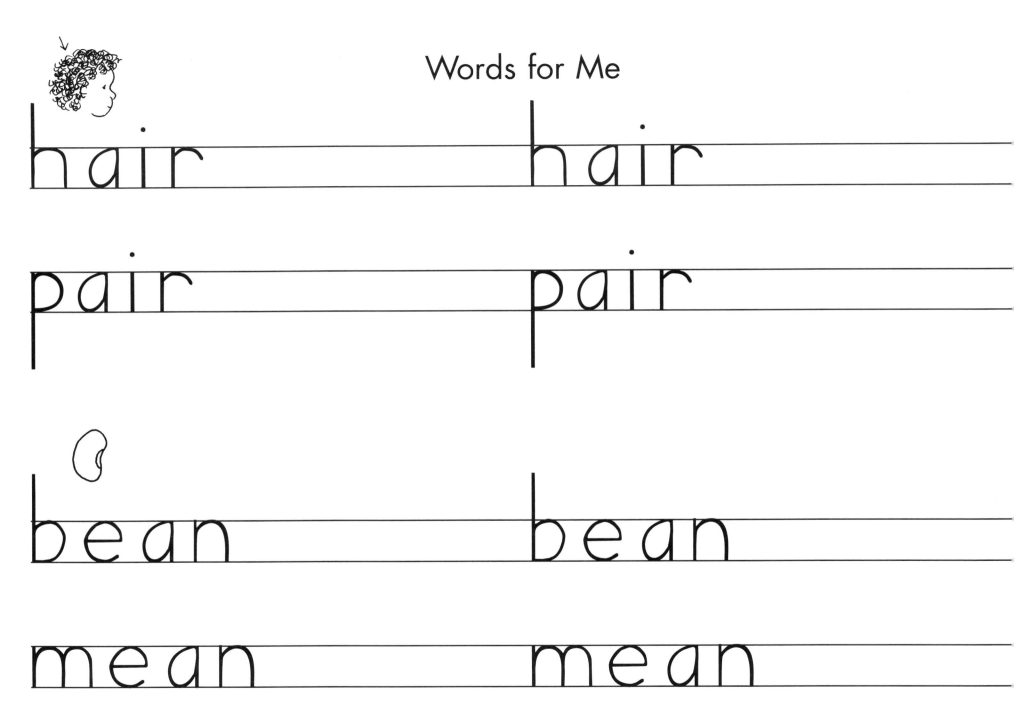

Words for Me

hair   hair

pair   pair

bean   bean

mean   mean

At first, curve up.
Then go straight down.

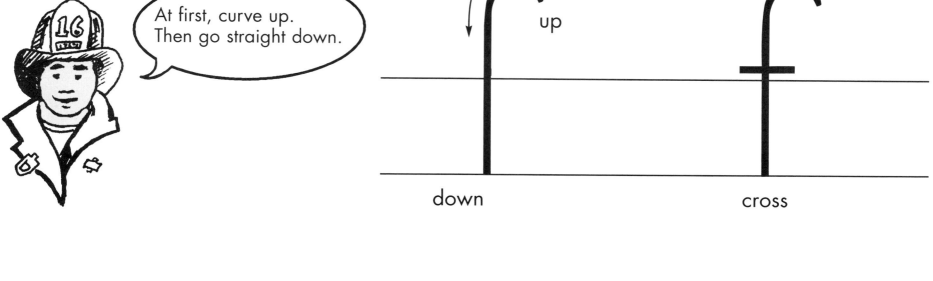

up

down   cross

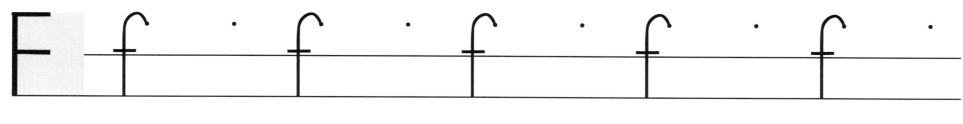

F

F is for **f**ish.

Magic c

bump

back down

up like a

U tu

Q q q q q q

Q is for **q**uilt.

78

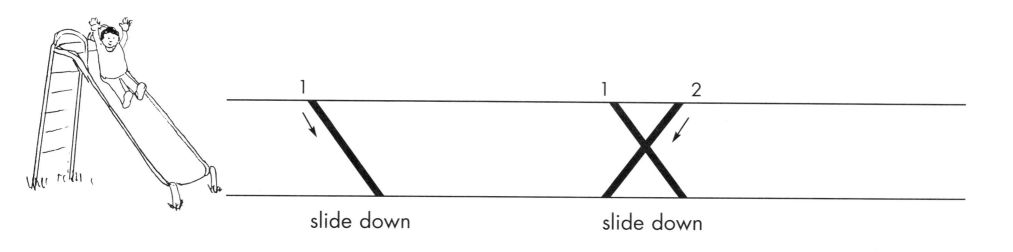

1

1   2

slide down   slide down

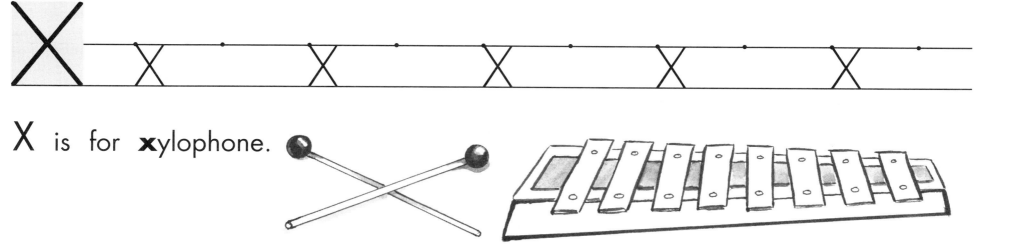

X is for **x**ylophone.

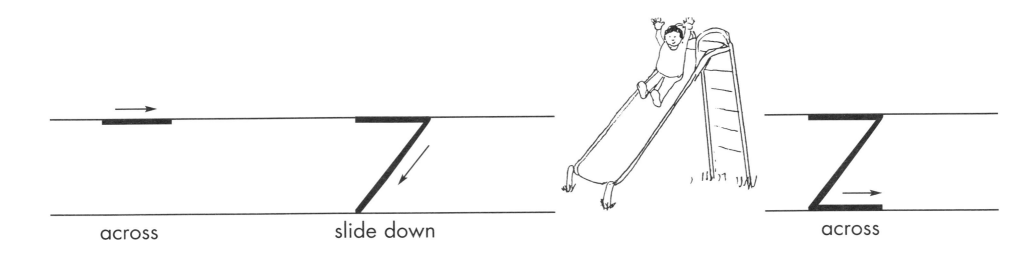

across   slide down   across

Z is for **z**ebra.

80

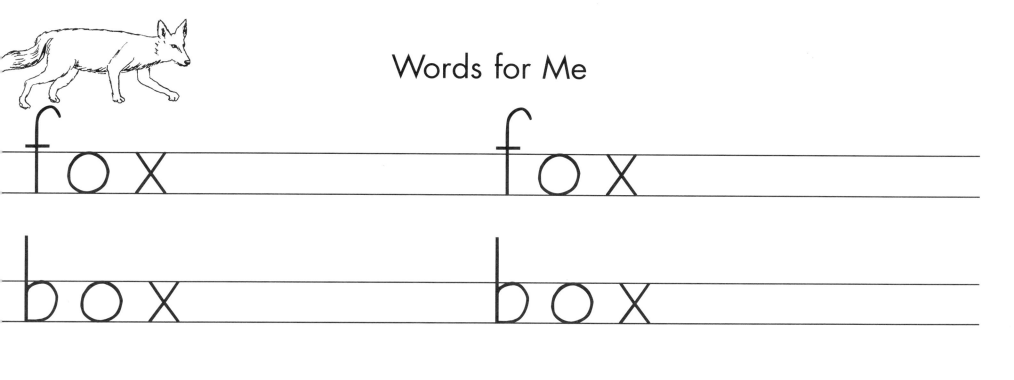

Words for Me

fox   fox

box   box

quiz   quiz

quit   quit

Fish swim.

I can write.

Extra large spaces are used for beginners.

Sentences for Me

Copy this page. Write sentences for your students to practice. Use extra large spaces between words.

My Name

Teacher should demonstrate and help each child learn how to write his or her name.